fabulous fizz

fabulous fizz

choosing champagne and sparkling wine for every occasion

alice king

photography by peter cassidy

TIME
LIFE
BOOKS

Alexandria, Virginia

Senior Designer Louise Leffler
Editors Jane Hughes, Maddalena Bastianelli
Picture and Location Researcher Kate Brunt
Production Patricia Harrington
Head of Design Gabriella Le Grazie
Publishing Director Anne Ryland

First published in the United Kingdom in 1999
by Ryland Peters & Small
Cavendish House,
51–55 Mortimer Street,
London W1N 7TD

10 9 8 7 6 5 4 3 2 1

Produced by Sun Fung Offset Binding Co., Ltd
Printed in China

Notes
All spoon measurements are level unless specified otherwise.
Ovens should be preheated to the specified temperature. If using a
fan-assisted oven, cooking times should be reduced accordingly.

*For my Father, who taught me to love
champagne and Debbie, who drinks almost
as much champagne as I do!*

Time-Life Books is a division of Time Life Inc.

TIME LIFE INC.
President and CEO: George Artandi

TIME-LIFE CUSTOM PUBLISHING
Vice President and Publisher   Terry Newell
Vice President of Sales and Marketing   Neil Levin
Director of Acquisitions and Editorial Resources   Jennifer Pearce
Director of Creative Services   Laura Ciccone McNeill
Director of Special Markets   Liz Ziehl
Project Manager   Jennie Halfant

TIME-LIFE is a trademark of Time Warner Inc. U.S.A.
Books produced by Time-Life Custom Publishing are available at a
special bulk discount for promotional and premium use. Custom
adaptations can also be created to meet your specific marketing goals.
Call 1-800-323-5255.

Library of Congress Cataloging-in-Publication Data
King, Alice, 1961–
Fabulous fizz / Alice King, with photograpy by Peter Cassidy.
p. cm.
Includes index.
ISBN 0–7370–2021–0
1. Champagne (Wine) 2. Sparkling wines. I. Peter Cassidy II. Title.
TP555.5.K56   1999
641.2'224--dc21CIP   99-26576

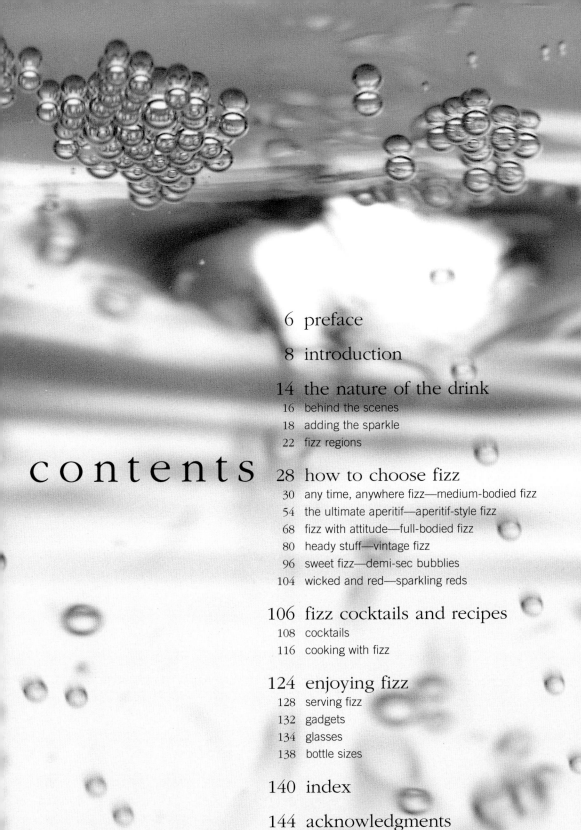

contents

This book is a celebration.
A celebration of a long love affair.
If you love life with a passion, you will love champagne.

preface

this book is a celebration. A celebration of a long love affair. If you love life with a passion, you will love champagne and other sparkling wines, as do I and all my best friends.

Fizz—as these fine wines are affectionately called—is the celebration drink. There is simply nothing that can compete with all those dancing bubbles and that wonderfully refreshing and seductive flavor. It is the froth of daydreams—the magic of its taste is a dream come true.

This bubbly affair of mine has been going on for some time. At age 18, I started what was for me the dream job—working as a guide in the cellars at Champagne Heidsieck Monopole, in the city of Reims. I learned lots of French and a lot more about the making, tasting, and, of course, the drinking of champagne. I was seduced.

One very special champagne celebration took place when my dream of having a baby at home came true with the birth of my third son, Felix. Within ten minutes of his arrival I drank a glass of Krug Grande Cuvée to celebrate, and it was one of the most magical and memorable moments in my life.

So I make no apologies for the fact that a great percentage of this book concentrates on champagne. For *Fabulous Fizz* is not a comprehensive guide to sparkling wine, more a personal view of some of the greatest fizzes in the world. And that includes some top-class sparklers made in countries as diverse as North America, Australia, Spain, and Italy.

But if I had to choose just one wine for my desert island? It would have to be that all-time favorite, fabulous fizz made in the north of France—champagne.

Alice King, June 1999

introduction

Celebratory, stylish, and frothy, fizz has been associated with fun for a long time—since the middle of the 17th century when London society first discovered the "uplifting" effect of this effervescing wine from Champagne. The Champagne region of France is the home of fizz; but sparkling wine is made in many other corners of the world, too—the Spanish enjoy bone-dry cava, the Italians love their gently sweet Asti, and the New World fizz regions—California, Australia, New Zealand, and South Africa—all make amazingly good fizz, too.

Just mention fizz and people's eyes will sparkle in anticipation. It's a fabulous tasting drink, with that wonderful bubbly sensation on the tongue. Served lightly chilled, streams of bubbles rise in the tall fluted glass. It might be pale golden in color, elegant and restrained in style, with hints of yeasty flavors. Or perhaps it's pale onion-pink, with heady aromas of strawberries; or maybe your ideal fizz is upfront and positively fruity. One of the many joys of sparkling wine is its wealth of styles—no matter what your taste buds prefer, there's a fizz for you. In this book, you'll discover non-vintage, vintage, dry and sweet fizzes, pink and even red fizzes. And, whatever the occasion, the celebratory style of this frothing wine means you can guarantee that it will be more than welcome.

My aim with this book is to pass on my enthusiasm for fabulous fizz. I have divided my favorite fizzes into three main sections—"any time, anywhere" medium-bodied fizzes, light aperitif-style, and then the richer styles that often show at their best with food. If you already have some firm fizz favorites, look them up in the index to see which section they fall into. Then you can go out and discover a whole host of other champagnes and sparkling wines of a similar style. But don't stop there; go on and experiment with others, too. There's a whole world of fabulous fizz to suit all palates, pockets, and occasions. If you aren't already a fizz fan, I guarantee you soon will be!

For instance, if you want an aperitif to mark the beginning of a special evening, try Champagne Pol Roger White Foil NV. This is a delicious fizz, with exotic hints of ginger and cream aromas and perfect balance. If you are having a laidback barbecue, you need an "any time, anywhere" kind of fizz to see you through, such as Seaview Brut Rosé NV or the fabulous Green Point, both from Australia. I am sure there will be those of you who, like me, will have no difficulty in enjoying more than a few glasses of the richer style of bubblies. The fabulously rich and creamy Krug Grande Cuvée NV takes pride of place in my roll call of "big" fizzes, while

HERE'S TO CHAMPAGNE, THE DRINK DIVINE THAT MAKES US FORGET OUR TROUBLES; IT'S MADE OF A DOLLAR'S WORTH OF WINE AND THREE DOLLARS' WORTH OF BUBBLES.

Anon.

California produces some fabulous rich fizzes that make great food partners, such as the buttery Korbel Chardonnay NV.

But when it comes to that big romance, or those very special, once-in-a-lifetime celebrations, then I suggest you splurge on vintage fizz. The wedding toast, for example, demands a fabulous fizz. You can do no better than the aptly named Iron Horse Wedding Cuvée 1996.

Fizz simply makes a party. The most fabulous party I have ever been to was, without doubt, the Champagne Piper Heidsieck bicentenary celebration in the mid-1980s. Held in the Orangerie and gardens at the Palace of Versailles just outside Paris, it was the most extravagant event that I have ever been to, with 1,600 guests invited for the launch of Piper Heidsieck's new deluxe cuvée, Champagne Rare. Entering the gardens as the sun set behind the lake, I watched the

fountains magically light up while an orchestra began playing Handel's *Water Music*. White-jacketed waiters were everywhere, each carrying magnums of champagne. Alongside the Piper Heidsieck Rare 1976, which although ten years old, was still youthful and crisp yet steely, with a wonderfully complex flavor, we were also offered magnums of Piper Heidsieck NV.

Even now, just one taste of Piper Heidsieck reminds me of the splendor of that grand evening, the long line of crisp white linen-covered tables spread with silver platters of food on each side of the Orangerie. There was every delicacy you could imagine, from roasted quails and quails' eggs to caviar, huge crayfish, crab, lobsters, and sizzling stir-fried duck. That was a truly magical evening, ending with a sensational firework display around the Lake of Versailles, and celebrated with bottles of very special champagnes.

But as my own party after the week of tasting bubbly contenders for *Fabulous Fizz* proved, there are plenty of fizzes for the not-so-grand and impromptu occasions, too! The bottles of fizz that I'd kept sparkling with trusty chrome champagne stoppers (see page 133) were stacked on ice in barrels all over the candlelit garden and in both bath tubs inside the house. The Wurlitzer jukebox played from dusk until dawn, and we dined on Chinese take-out cooked by Damien who runs the local Chinese delivery van. We discovered some great fizzes and some delicious combinations to drink with the Singapore noodles, vegetables with black bean sauce, chicken with water chestnuts and bean sprouts, and beef with ginger and garlic. It was the best party I have ever held, and I owe it all to the fabulous fizz!

The inevitable result of tasting all these fizzes was not a hangover, but an excess of champagne corks. As it was Christmas time, I simply used them as tree decorations, spraying them silver and hanging them on the tree by their wires. It looked very pretty and made everyone smile. There are no doubt 101 other uses for a popped champagne cork, but one of my favorites is to make a memento for a godchild. Keep one of the corks from the fizz served at the christening party, cut a hole in its base, and insert a silver coin. I also have a friend who keeps the corks from the first bottle of fizz she shares with her lovers. I choose not to count them!

Even the bottle itself, particularly a magnum of champagne, can add to the sense of occasion. Yielding to one of those impulsive desires recently, I opened a bottle of Veuve Clicquot La Grande Dame 1990 to share with a friend who is very label-conscious. Even before tasting it, he remarked that this must be a very classy fizz, because of its stylish, old-fashioned shape and its seal. He was right, this is immensely elegant champagne! At the other extreme are designer bottles like the minimalist "J," from California producer Jordan, with its very eye-catching green and yellow "J" logo. It's a very fine fizz, too, with creamy, toasty, biscuity aromas and flavors.

Sparkling wine also makes for both eye-catching and really tasty cocktails (see pages 108–115). The simplest of all and a great choice to order at a restaurant, bar or club is a Kir Royale, refreshing, fruity with a hint of blackcurrant, and very stylish, too.

If there's one thing that beats a glass of fizz, it's enjoying fizz with food. And I don't just mean at a dinner party, it can just as easily be brunch, a barbecue, an early supper with your workmates; any meal can be turned into a special occasion with a glass of sparkling wine. The richer styles of fizz—the vintage sparklers, prestige

cuvées, and the full-bodied rosés in particular—really come into their own with food. They have the weight, the structure, the sheer complexity of character to complement even the richest of creamy sauces and the strongest of spicy flavors.

The most obvious occasion at which fizz is the star is a party or reception, where hopefully the trays of canapés will come your way more than once. Tasty nibbles can range from salty nuts and garlicky olives through to mini mozzarella and tomato tartlets. What you need is a refreshing, crisp and fruity fizz to partner all those flavors. Try an elegant aperitif-style bubbly, or an affordable, easy-drinking "any time" sparkler.

If you really want to impress your guests, serve them a richer style of fizz as an aperitif—it will whet their appetite too—and continue to pour it with the first course. How about serving Wild Mushroom and Champagne Risotto (see page 118)? Those bold, earthy, creamy flavors will really be enhanced by a rich, biscuity champagne. Or try a rich fizz with creamy asparagus soup. For a truly fabulous meal, serve sparkling wine throughout. Fizz is just

perfect with fish, particularly with the richer, meatier fish such as sea bass, turbot, or monkfish. One of my favorite suppers is a glass or two of fizz with roasted cod steaks in a spicy tomato sauce. As for fizz and seafood, such as lobster and fresh crab, it's a match made in heaven as far as I'm concerned.

It surprised me, too, the first time I tried it, but fizz with red meat is actually extremely good. In fact, there's a whole host of dishes you can enjoy with sparkling wine—anything from spicy Indian dishes to Thai noodles, and scallops with ginger to garlicky chargrilled chicken wings. When it comes to dessert, a demi-sec bubbly can transform even something as simple as homemade fruit ice cream or sherbet served with tiny almond cookies into a sublime experience. I think the extra prickle of the bubble on the tongue and the citruslike acidity mean that demi-sec fizzes really can cut through the richness of desserts.

As you'll discover in this book, there are lots of wonderful combinations to experiment and some delicious recipes to try out. So why choose anything other than fabulous fizz?

the nature of fizz

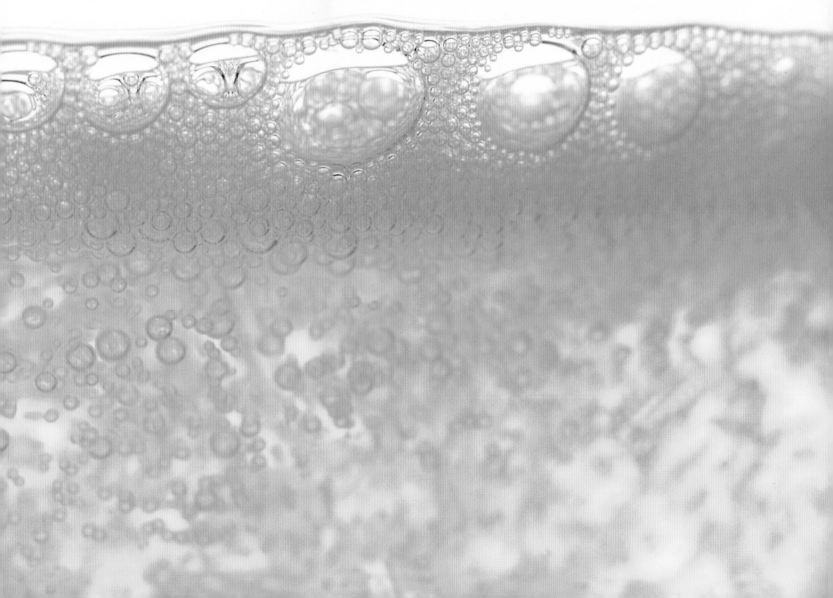

Have you ever played that game where most like to invite to dinner? Top of

Fun and frivolous, fizz has long been in demand by partygoers. From the 17th-century café society to the "roaring" 1920s and on, fizz has been *the* celebratory drink, as these fabulous French posters from the 1920s all too clearly show!

you have to choose six guests, living or dead, whom you would
~~~~y list would be the 17th-century French monk, Dom Pérignon.

behind the scenes

Champagne has been around for centuries, but only since the close of the 1600s has it been intentionally fizzy. Before then it was a fairly thin, acidic still wine that would sometimes irritatingly decide to start fermenting again in the bottle, causing more than a few explosions. Then, in the mid 1700s, the fashionable café society in London took a fancy to the fizzy version; one thing led to another, and it was discovered that adding a judicial spoonful of sugar would cause a second fermentation and result in those magical bubbles on demand. By the turn of the 18th century, champagne sparkled.

Have you ever played that game where you have to decide on six guests, living or dead, whom you would like to invite to dinner? Whom would you invite? Top of my list would be Dom Pérignon, a French monk who played a key role in creating what has become my favorite drink. Mind you, it would be quite a costly dinner, as I'd have to serve him Moët & Chandon's vintage prestige cuvée, Dom Pérignon, a truly fabulous fizz!

Appointed treasurer at the Abbey of Hautvilliers just outside Epernay in Champagne in 1668, the blessed monk's duties included winemaking. For a long time he was believed to have been the one who "invented" sparkling champagne. Although that particular claim to fame is no longer attributed to him, Dom Pérignon introduced some incredibly innovative winemaking techniques, including the art of blending wines from different vineyards to get the best results, and making a white wine out of black grapes. Both these processes remain central to the way fizz is made today.

Another great figure in champagne's history is the formidable Nicole-Barbe Clicquot-Ponsardin. Widowed while still in her 20s, she took over the running of her husband's business in 1805 and created what has become one of the most famous champagne houses, Veuve Clicquot Ponsardin. Besides the fact that she was a very successful businesswoman in a man's world 200 years ago, the "Grande Dame" claimed immortality through the development of the extraordinary *remuage* process (see page 19).

Throughout the 1800s, as demand for this fabulous fizz spread across Europe, new houses were set up with names such as Bollinger, Louis Roederer, Perrier-Jouët. The methods by which champagne is now produced were developed and perfected. Champagne became the celebrated drink of the aristocracy. It was drunk at all fashionable Parisian parties, at the Regency Court at Versailles, it was shipped to the Czar in Russia, and demanded by the elite of London society.

As the 21st century opens, this celebratory drink continues to hold sway. What has changed is the variety of sparkling wines on offer—not only Champagne from France, but cava from Spain, Asti from Italy, and of course those fabulous fizzes from North America, Australia, and New Zealand. I find it incredible to think that it is only in the past ten years or so that "New World" sparkling wines have really become international stars. In such a short time, producers have taken some breathtaking leaps to catch up with the 300 years of experience enjoyed by the Champenois. Which gives us all a wealth of fabulous fizzes from which to choose...

adding the sparkle

The yeast eats up the sugar and burps out tiny bubbles of carbon dioxide

The majority of fabulous fizzes, be they champagnes or sparkling wines from around the world, are made using the *méthode champenoise* (called *méthode traditionelle* or, more simply, "bottle-fermented" outside Champagne). This involves a fascinating, lengthy, and tricky process and is one of the reasons why good fizz will never be cheap.

the champagne way

At first fizz is made like any still wine. The grapes are picked, pressed, and fermented, usually in polished-steel vats, although some producers use oak. The resulting wine is still and in colder regions such as Champagne, it tends to be quite acidic and pale. This is where the magic begins. First comes the blending, an art form in itself that ensures that the quality and "house style" of the fizz is consistent. The winemaker tastes wines from the vats of separately fermented juices from individual vineyards and areas and decides on the exact proportions, or *assemblage,* of each that will go into the final blend. The blended wine is then bottled and given a dose of yeast and sugar, which causes the crucial second fermentation. The most imaginative explanation I've been given of what happens during this fermentation is that the yeast eats up the sugar and in effect burps out tiny bubbles of carbon dioxide that remain trapped in the wine, creating a fabulously frothing fizz.

Depending on the quality and style of fizz, the wine will now be left "on its yeast lees" for anything from a few weeks to several months to allow those yeasty, biscuity, rich aromas and flavors that we associate with fabulous fizz to develop. Then comes the tricky bit. How to remove those tiny dead yeast cells from the wine (leaving it clear) without losing the streams of bubbles? This is where the second magician, the *remueur*, or riddler, as we'd call him in English, appears. The bottles are placed horizontally, neck first, in hinged wooden racks that are kept in the coolest, darkest part of the cellars. Once a day for about two months, each bottle is twisted and tipped up slightly, a process that is known as *remuage*. This gentle disturbance loosens the yeast sediment, and it gradually slips into the neck of the bottle, which, by the end of the two months is virtually upside-down in the rack. Amazingly skilled riddlers can turn up to 40,000 bottles a day! The *remuage* is now mainly done by large computer-operated cages called *gyropalettes*, although most prestige cuvées made in Champagne are still riddled by hand.

The necks of the bottles are then gently lowered into a freezing solution causing an ice plug to form around the yeast sediment. If you are lucky enough to be visiting a sparkling wine cellar while this is happening, it's great drama to watch the *dégorgement*, as the cork is removed and the ice plug shoots spectacularly out of the bottle. Inevitably, a little fizz is lost, too, so the bottle is quickly topped up with the *dosage*, a quantity of older wine and a small amount of sugar. Even the brut, or dry fizzes, are given a small dose of sugar, which is added to balance the acidity that keeps the fizz fresh as it matures.

Finally the fizz is sealed with the famous Champagne cork and wire. The wire muzzle prevents the cork from popping out, since the pressure within the bottle is quite something (at least comparable to the pressure in a large truck tire). Good-quality fizzes are then kept in the cellar for at least six months before being released.

alternative methods

There are other ways of adding bubbles to sparkling wine. The most successful of these is the *cuve close* or "tank method," where the second fermentation takes place in a large, sealed tank. As the amount of wine in contact with the yeast is considerably less, these wines tend to lack the complexity of flavor of bottle-fermented fizzes. The quickest, simplest, and crudest method of making sparkling wine, and the one used to make some of the cheapest fizzes around, is simply to pump carbon dioxide through the wine (the way fizzy soft drinks are made). It is relatively easy to detect a carbonated sparkling wine since the bubbles tend to be much bigger and the wine loses its fizz extremely quickly.

making it pink

To make pink fizz, you have two choices: traditionally, the skins of black grapes are left with the juice after pressing and this "dyes" the juice, or else red wine is added until the juice is sufficiently pink. Rosés come in all shades of pink, from pale onion-skin pink to a deep reddish pink.

that remain trapped in the wine, creating that fabulously frothing fizz...

fizz grapes, terms, and style

grapes

Most fabulous fizzes, be they white or rosé, are made from a blend of Pinot Noir and Chardonnay grapes. The third "classic champagne grape" is Pinot Meunier. But that's not the whole story. As you'll discover in this book, there are stunning champagnes and sparkling wines made from just Chardonnay, or from a blend of the two Pinots, not to mention blends of other grapes. And there's also some fabulous sparkling wine made from grape varieties such as Muscat and Shiraz (see fizz regions, pages 22–27).

chardonnay

The importance of this white grape when it comes to sparkling wine is that it brings elegance to the fizz; it's the subtle balance of complexity and refined fruit flavor that make Chardonnay such a star performer. It is also believed to have the greatest potential for aging of the three grapes. A young Chardonnay wine is light and flowery and has a fresh, citruslike vibrant edge with good acidity; with several years' bottle age it becomes fatter, developing richer, buttery, creamy flavors.

pinot noir

The winsome Pinot Noir adds weight and body—the "backbone," if you like—and finesse to the blend. And, as an enticing extra, it brings the delicious mouth-watering flavors of strawberries and raspberries. Fizzes made with Pinot Noir sometimes have an attractive, very slight pale-pink tinge from the brief contact of the juice with the black skins during pressing.

pinot meunier

Don't underestimate Pinot Meunier; this black grape is an essential addition to the blend in champagne, particularly for the nonvintage fizzes. It is wonderfully fruity, rather like hard candy, with a hint of spice, and it brings an easy-drinking style to the wine. Outside the Champagne region, this is the variety that tends to be dropped from the team.

terms and styles

There are certain terms on fizz labels that can give you a clue as to the style or flavor of the dancing bubbles inside. These are some of the most widely used.

méthode champenoise/ bottle-fermented

The all-important clue as to how those bubbles got in the bottle. This is the method used in Champagne, meaning that the second fermentation takes place in the bottle (see page 19). Look for the terms *méthode traditionelle*, "traditional method," or "bottle-fermented" on fizzes made outside Champagne.

nonvintage (NV)

One of my favorite styles of fizz. Nonvintage fizzes are made from a blend of wines from several years to achieve a consistency of "house style" and quality. This means that once you find a nonvintage fizz to your liking, you should be able to buy it any time, anywhere, safe in the knowledge that it will always be as you expect. With several years of bottle age (if you can resist drinking them), these bubblies become softer, richer, and creamier.

vintage

A wine from a single year. The best producers reserve the finest fruit for vintage fizz, which is one good reason why it's so desirable. A vintage sparkler will reflect as much of the character of the vintage as it does of the producer, and so may taste quite different from one year to the next. For example, a fizz made in a very hot year will taste much richer, rounder, and less acidic than a fizz produced in a cooler year. In colder, wetter regions such as Champagne, the top vintage fizzes are only made in years when the quality of the grapes is considered special enough. Happily, more often than not. Most good champagne houses will age their vintage champagnes for five to seven years before release.

blanc de blancs

Literally translated this means "white of white," which tells you that the fizz is made using only the Chardonnay grape. When young, these wines can be relatively light, delicate and creamy; with a little more age, *blanc de blancs* fizzes often develop a fabulously rich, toasted, biscuity flavor.

blanc de noirs

Although "white of black" may sound like a contradiction in terms, it's not. What it tells you is that the fizz has been made using only black grapes i.e. Pinot Noir and Pinot Meunier. And no, you don't have to be a magician to do this. Just cut a black grape in half—it is only the skin that is black, not the pulp. So as long as you take the juice away from the skins quickly after pressing, a white wine can be made using black grapes. A fizz made from black grapes only is always full-bodied and rich.

prestige cuvées/deluxe cuvées

These are the top-of-the-line blends (i.e. cuvées), the really fabulous fizzes with style and quality, to be savored on special occasions, high days, and holidays. Both vintage and nonvintage, prestige cuvées are luxury champagnes. They taste truly sublime and you can expect to pay for the privilege.

brut (brut réserve)

This is the style of fizz you'll find most often. Very popular, very drinkable, and usually nonvintage, these are "dry" fizzes, although they do in fact have a touch of balancing sugar in them, which helps makes them so palatable and delicious. (A style not often seen is brut zéro/ultra brut. This is tartly bone-dry as it has had no sugar added with the *dosage* [see page 19]. I find this style of fizz tastes rather sour and metallic.)

demi-sec

Just to confuse you, although the translation of *demi-sec* is "half dry," the best way to describe these delectable fizzes is "half sweet," because that's just what they are—a wonderful balance of honeyed sweetness and refreshing acidity.

crémant

When you see the word "crémant" on a bottle label, for example Crémant d'Alsace and Crémant de Loire, it tells you this is a soft, creamy sparkling wine, less fizzy than champagne. A wine that is gently bubbly rather than furiously fizzy—an example would be the Italian sparkler Asti Spumante—may be described as *pétillant*, or as having a light "spritz."

This is a quick tour to introduce you to some of the finest sparkling wine regions in the world, the sources of the fabulous fizzes included in this book. They include the famous, the up-and-coming, and the lesser-known places where I've discovered some real gems. If you get the chance to visit, you'll find a number of producers are geared up for visitors and will give you a warm welcome and often a refreshing glass of their fabulous fizz.

france: champagne

Just what is it about this corner of northern France that makes its wines so fabulous? There are those who say the secret lies in the soil, that it is the underlying chalk that imparts such a special character to the grapes. Then there are the grapes themselves, the three classic varieties from which champagne is made (no others are permitted): Chardonnay, Pinot Noir, and Pinot Meunier (see page 20). Then, of course, there is the climate to consider. It's relatively cold and certainly wet. But this is to the advantage of champagne: the less sun, the more acidity, and vines that have to struggle for some reason will produce delicate fruit with pure yet intense flavors. This is exactly what's needed to create fabulous fizz. And I'd better not forget the human touch, especially the crucial skills of the blender!

fizz regions

It's really a combination of all these factors, plus the carefully upheld traditions and a sprinkling of magic that makes champagne, for me, still far and away the greatest fizz in the world. The French are very possessive about their unique sparkling heritage. The very name "Champagne" is almost sanctified—no one outside the region may use it on any product or for any purpose.

The Comité Interprofessionel des Vins de Champagne (CIVC), the governing body that looks after the champagne industry, is quite prepared to take companies to court to protect the name. The fashion house of Yves St. Laurent for one was forced to withdraw a perfume it had named "Champagne" (did the CIVC really think we'd mistake the two, or be tempted to drink the perfume?!).

The names that roll off the tongue and are most familiar to us, such as Moët & Chandon, Taittinger, and Louis Roederer, are the big houses, many of which you can visit. It makes a really special weekend trip, especially in the fall when the vines have turned the hillsides golden-brown. If you stay in Epernay, in the heart of the vineyards, you can walk from one house to the next, enjoying a glass or two of fizz and exploring the underground cellars. These are an impressive sight: miles and miles of cold, slightly damp tunnels—even a cavernous room at Champagne Mercier

that is used for grand banquets—that were dug out of the chalk centuries ago in Gallo-Roman times, and are now filled with bottles of fizz. My idea of heaven.

loire valley

The Loire Valley has a long tradition of sparkling wine production. Indeed, Saumur producers claim to have been in the fizz business long before the Champenois. The two styles of fizz to look out for here are sparkling Saumur and Vouvray. Made predominantly from the main grape of the Loire, Chenin Blanc, these are gently sparkling wines with an unusual, soft, elderflower flavor that becomes distinctly more earthy and honeyed as the wine ages. The best sparkling Saumurs and Vouvrays are refreshingly crisp, ideal for summertime parties. Since the appellation was created in 1976, the quality of these wines has improved since small growers now make the fizz with care.

alsace

Compared to the fizzes of the Loire and Champagne, Crémant d'Alsace is a very recent creation. Bottle-fermented fizz was introduced by one of the region's top producers, Dopff "au Moulin." The main grape variety is Pinot Blanc, and some Chardonnay makes an appearance. The few good Crémants d'Alsace I've found have a nutty flavor and crisp style.

Miles and miles of cold, slightly damp tunnels, filled with bottles of champagne—my idea of heaven.

limoux

Blanquette de Limoux is a little-known fizzy gem that I discovered, tucked away in the hinterland of the Languedoc region, in the south of France. Made from the aromatic Mauzac grape, the best blanquettes have wonderful honeyed, spicy aromas and flavors as well as an attractive earthy character. These distinctive fizzes are technically "brut," or dry, yet the perfumed nature of the grape gives an attractive impression of sweetness on the palate.

spain

Spain's fabulous fizz is known as cava and is unbelievably good value. Most of it is made in the Penedés region of Catalonia, traditionally using three grape varieties, Macabeo, Parellada, and Xarel-lo. As with the grapes used in champagne, each is considered to bring a particular characteristic to the wine. That said, Chardonnay is playing an increasingly dominant role, so when you see a "blanc de blancs" cava, this tells you it's made from Chardonnay. Cava has a very distinctive flavor. It's certainly much softer than champagne, with less perceivable acidity, and a lightly floral, sometimes smoky flavor.

italy

The classic Italian sparklers, Asti Spumante and Moscato d'Asti, come from Piedmont in northern Italy and are named after the local hilltop town of Asti. They are both made from the Muscat (*Moscato* in Italian) grape, which, though it sounds strange, is best described as "grapey"! These are wonderfully easy-drinking, softly sparkling fizzes, lower in alcohol (around 7%), very attractively perfumed, and with deliciously fresh, green grape flavors. They are also gently sweet, yet with that thirst-quenching tang of citrussy acidity on the finish. Of the two, Moscato d'Asti is the finer fizz and more consistent in quality.

united kingdom

Ten years ago, I would never have dreamed that English wines could in any way be described as "fabulous." Such is the leap forward in winemaking and planting of better-quality grapes, including Chardonnay, that there are now several quite stunning sparkling wines. It makes sense; after all, the UK has a "cool" climate, and there are chalky soils across southeastern England, just as there are in Champagne...

united states

As a novice journalist, aged 21, I was sent by UK wine magazine *Decanter* to interview a reader at his rather grand home. I was offered a glass of fizz, which I very happily accepted. It was rich and creamy with the most wonderful raspberry and cream overtones. Having spent a spell working in the Champagne region, I thought I knew a thing or two about fizz, and presumed we were drinking some

serious vintage champagne. Wrong! I was amazed to learn we were drinking California fizz, a sensationally complex Schramsberg Blanc de Noirs from one of California's top sparkling wine producers. It was in fact Schramsberg who began the whole sparkling wine trend in the States back in 1965, concentrating on making fizz from Chardonnay, Pinot Noir, and Pinot Blanc. These fizzes swiftly became the models that all others aspired to equal.

California now heads the list of sparkling wine states in the U.S., closely shadowed in terms of quality if not quantity by her Pacific Northwest neighbors—witness the excellent Argyle from Oregon and the fizzes from Château Ste-Michelle in Washington State—with New York State representing the East Coast. Chardonnay and Pinot Noir have been planted in the best sites to get that all-important tangy acidity and finesse of character. Carneros, Sonoma, and Mendocino Counties are now home to some of the best known and fabulous of California's fizzes, wines that positively burst with mouth-watering, upfront fruit. The Champenois were also quick to jump on the fizz bandwagon. Today companies including Moët & Chandon (Domaine Chandon), Mumm, and Taittinger (Domaine Carneros) all have major sparkling wine interests in California. So, too, do the cava producers Freixenet (Gloria Ferrer) and Codorníu.

australia

Australia is a must for any fan of fabulous fizz. Rather like the still wines from this huge and prolific grape-growing continent, Australia's sparkling wines offer huge diversity. It gets a big thumbs-up from me for the very affordable, easy-drinking, everyday party bubblies, not to mention the stunningly classy rich fizzes that are grand enough for the chicest occasions. As for the unique sparkling reds, mostly made from the spicy, fruity Shiraz grape, these have to be tasted to be believed.

While Australia can trace its sparkling wine history back over 100 years, its current thriving industry really kicked in around the same time as California's, when the world woke up to this fabulous drink and wanted more of these refreshing bubblies. The astute Aussie winemakers sought out the coolest areas, such as Great Western, in Victoria, and planted the classic Champagne grapes. The top sparklers are mostly Chardonnay/Pinot Noir blends, while the easy-drinking, fruity fizzes for those "any time" moments can be blends of a number of grape varieties.

Again, the Champenois spotted a good thing, and in the 1980s Moët & Chandon flew in and set up Domaine Chandon at Green Point, in the Yarra Valley, Victoria. Green Point, along with the Aussie Seaview and Seppelt fizzes, represent fantastic value in the middle price bracket.

A relative newcomer to the fizz stakes, once started it seems there's no stopping New Zealand. The fizzes are crisp and dry, with wonderful finesse and style.

new zealand

A relative newcomer to the fizz stakes, once started it seems there's no stopping New Zealand. The bubblies are currently going from strength to strength, exhibiting depths of flavor that even ten years ago would have been unthinkable. All good news for fizz lovers! In terms of style and taste, the biggest compliment I can pay New Zealand fizz is that I can be hard pressed to differentiate between top New Zealand fizz and the best of Champagne. New Zealand fizzes are crisp and dry, with a wonderful finesse and style. The leading producers are based on the South Island, in the cool—and inevitably wet—Marlborough region, where, fortunately for us, the somewhat bland and widely planted Müller-Thurgau grape was ignored in favor of Chardonnay and Pinot Noir. The Champenois, never a breed to miss a trick or two, also recognized the potential for fabulous fizz. Which is why Champagne Deutz joined up with Marlborough-based Montana (who independently make consistently good-quality, distinguished fizzes), invested a heap of money, and promptly produced the stunning Marlborough Deutz sparklers.

south africa

While quite a lot of South Africa's sparkling wine is made using the *cuve close* method (see page 19), which luckily for us is generally consumed within South Africa, a number of startlingly good bottle-fermented fizzes have begun to emerge. The South Africans have introduced their own sparkling wine term, Méthode Cap Classique, for these fizzes. The future looks temptingly promising, with some delicate, well-structured wines making their presence felt beyond the borders of the Cape. And what better indicator of this promise than the fact that the champagne house of Mumm has already teamed up with one of the finest stars in this still tiny industry to produce Cuvée Cap by Mumm?

how to choose fizz

any time, anywhere fizz

Medium-bodied, approachable, and easy-drinking fizzes, with lots of upfront fruit, some richness, well-balanced, and full of flavor. Great food fizzes.

the joy of the fizzes I've selected for this section is that they are extremely versatile. Unlike the richer, heavier styles of fizz where a glass or two can be enough, these wines will see you through wherever you are and however long it lasts. Whether it's partying or lunching with friends, these fizzes will add just that touch of sparkle to all kinds of occasions. The growing trend for wine by the glass in bars and clubs means that it is easier to indulge in a glass of fizz without splurging on a whole bottle. It's also a great way to discover some new fizzes... Should you know someone who's not keen on fizz, you can guarantee to convert them in no time at all with one of these fun and fizzy "any time, anywhere" wines.

These sparkling wines are very easy to drink; they just slip down beautifully. The added advantage is that they tend to be more widely available and offer great value for the money, too. What's more, they are great with food, having enough "weight," body, and depth of flavor to cope. Champagne Billecart-Salmon Brut Réserve NV with sea bass in a light cream and vanilla sauce is heavenly. And if you're munching a homemade hamburger with a pile of hot fries, what other than an American bestseller—Korbel Brut NV?

breakfast and brunch

There's something wonderfully decadent about sipping bubbly at breakfast time. Imagine the smell of freshly brewed coffee and the sight of toasted muffins and scrambled eggs with smoked salmon. Why not spoil yourself and crack open a bottle of fizz? Even if you don't have friends around, do you really need an excuse to indulge on a Sunday morning? I'm all for it! The clean, refreshing flavors of these medium-bodied fizzes, with their crisp acidity, are ideal to cut through the morning fuzz—and the creamy eggs. If you prefer something refreshing and revitalizing, pour a little fizz into a glass of orange juice and add a dash of Grenadine to make Buck's Fizz (see page 109). For the best flavor, it is important to use freshly squeezed orange juice. For a special breakfast or brunch fizz, you can do no better than Champagne Perrier-Jouët NV. It has attractive balance, and lots of tangy fruit with a light vanilla finish. The lively S. Anderson Napa Valley Brut NV, with its tinglingly refreshing lemon-citrussy character, is a great California brunch fizz.

For more breakfast fizz suggestions, see page 90

on the town

Meeting up with friends at the end of a hard week at the office? Stopping off at your favorite bar for a quick drink and gossip? Start the evening in style with a glass or two of fizz. Go for wines with some body and weight and fruit character, something you can really savor and enjoy. I've found Champagne Gosset Brut Excellence NV, with its toasted aroma and tangy fruit, works wonders at getting everyone into the mood; and those bubbles are a wonderful reminder that the fun has started. The spicy apricot and sherbet overtones of the California Korbel Brut NV make it a winner every time. Why not try the house fizz if you know the place and enjoy the wines? And if you decide to order some food, hang onto that glass of fizz.

For more "on the town" fizz suggestions, see page 56

staying in

Curled up on the sofa with a good movie and take-out—do you really need more of an excuse to share a bottle of fizz? After all, these are drink-me any time anywhere fizzes, and sparkling wine is surprisingly good with Chinese noodles and spicy foods, not to mention fish and chips! Two great-value fizzes to pick up on the way home are the easy-drinking Angus Brut Pinot Noir Chardonnay NV from Australia and the Spanish Castell 1909 Cava NV. This relatively full-bodied cava, with its hint of licorice and tangy yet creamy flavor on the finish, tastes exceptionally good with lots of foreign dishes.

Here's a fail-safe recipe for those moments when you need pampering or cheering up. Pour a glass of fabulous fizz such as the Champagne Billecart-Salmon Rosé NV, with its delicate vanilla aroma and delicious mouthful of strawberries and cream. Now put on some favorite music. One of my favorite pieces, which always makes me laugh out loud, is Strauss's *The Champagne Polka*, complete with authentic-sounding popping corks.

For more "staying in" fizz suggestions, see page 56

lunch

A glass of fizz can turn a simple lunch into a sparkly affair. After a morning's hard shopping, treat yourself to some bubbles with that plate of smoked salmon or stir-fried noodles. Gloria Ferrer Blanc de Noirs NV is a very sensational fizz from California. Pale pink in color, with red-fruit flavors, this is a great way to start a leisurely lunch. The elegant Mumm de Cramant Grand Cru NV, with its toasty, buttery flavor, will slip down beautifully with salmon served in a variety of guises. The nonvintage Lindauer Special Reserve from New Zealand, with its unusual and attractive yeasty, slightly biscuity edge, makes a refreshing, gently uplifting lunchtime sparkler, while you can't go wrong with Angus Brut Rosé NV, a great everyday pink fizz from Australia.

For more lunchtime fizz suggestions, see pages 61 and 75

seduction

Domaine Carneros NV is a top-quality Californian sparkling wine that needs to be tasted to be believed. Made in conjunction with the champagne house Taittinger, this is a really delicious fizz with

One of my favorite
Australian fizzes at
the moment is the
raspberry and vanilla-
tasting Yalumba
Cuvée One Pinot Noir
Chardonnay NV.

a creamy aroma and lots of red-fruit flavor. As my tasting notes on this fizz read, "it has an extremely seductive aftertaste;" this could well be one to pick if you have a hot new date! Billecart-Salmon Brut Réserve NV is an immensely classy champagne, with a subtle and complex, creamy vanilla aroma. The combination of a chilled glass of this elegant fizz served with oysters in a shallot and vinegar dressing is exquisite, and, yes, I most certainly believe that together they are one of the most powerful aphrodisiacs around!

One very persuasive fizz to come out of South Africa is Cabriere Estate's Pierre Jourdan Cuvée Belle Rose NV. Made from 100% Pinot Noir, it has just the faintest hint of pink, luscious soft fruit and a crisp finish. Lindauer Special Reserve NV is a great wine to serve at an intimate gathering when there's just the two of you—or any time when you want a relatively special sparkler to linger over without breaking the bank. This is one of New Zealand's most consistently good fizzes.

For more seductive fizz suggestions, see pages 58 and 84

For two intimates, lovers or comrades, to spend a quiet evening with a magnum, drinking no aperitif before, nothing but a glass of cognac after—that is the ideal.

... The worst time is that dictated by convention, in a crowd, in the early afternoon, at a wedding reception. Evelyn Waugh, *New York Vogue*, 1937

parties

All the best parties I have ever been to revolved around fizz. You don't, of course, have to have such a grand setting as Versailles (see page 10) for a fabulous party. But something about that pop of the cork really does conjure up an immediate party atmosphere, however informal or chic the setting. There is simply nothing like getting high on sparkling wine, and what you'll notice at fizz-only parties is that the bubble doesn't seem to burst. I'm also convinced that if you stick to drinking only good fizz, you won't get a hangover.

There are lots of cool new happening drinks around, but if you are throwing a big birthday party, serving fizz and only fizz throughout has to be the coolest choice of all. A medium-bodied, fruity sparkling wine with a gentle acidity will be a very popular choice. Seaview Brut NV from Australia, with its slightly smoky aroma and gentle fruit, is a great inexpensive choice, particularly for big parties, while

the easy-drinking, crisply acid Korbel Brut NV is a good all-rounder. If your budget is more generous, the delicious ice-cream-soda flavored Champagne Mumm Cordon Rouge NV makes the perfect party fizz.

For parties where the emphasis is on food, especially if it includes seafood such as shrimp or the more glamorous oysters, you cannot beat a decent bottle of medium-bodied champagne. Veuve Clicquot Yellow Label NV, with its stylish yeasty aroma and creamy fruit, is a great foil for oysters. They were made for each other. If you like the thought of champagne with a slightly toasted aroma, then serve Gosset Grande Réserve NV. It has lots of apricots and peachy flavors and a lovely tang of tropical fruit on the finish. As with many good nonvintage champagnes, stash a few bottles away (if you can resist drinking them), and they will become richer still over the next few years. My next suggestion is not champagne, but it will look good, impress your guests, and flatter the food. It's another of my favorite Australian fizzes, the raspberry and vanilla-tasting Yalumba Cuvée One Pinot Noir Chardonnay NV. I always think its packaging looks a bit like the Champagne Bollinger RD Label; the fizz is almost as complex and classy, too.

For more party fizz suggestions, see pages 61, 71, and 85

outside/bbqs

If you have friends coming for a barbecue, keep them entertained while the charcoal heats up by serving good, easy-drinking bubbly. The Aussies are, of course, masters of the barbecue, so it makes sense to me to serve some Australian fizz. One of my favorites is Green Point, a wine made in conjunction with the champagne

The Nineties, the "Gay Nineties," were the peak period of the popularity of Champagne in England. There was peace and plenty, profits and prospects for all and sundry as never before or since... What other wine than Champagne could be ordered on festive occasions, the gay foil of the bottle, the merry popping of the cork, the dancing bubbles in the glass helped all alike, making guests happy and articulate, hence the party a success.

André Simon, *Vintagewise*

house Moët & Chandon. While Green Point is a vintage wine (at the time of writing the vintage is 1995; see also vintage fizzes, pages 80–95), it is consistently good, with a lovely, intense, slightly toasted aroma, and excellent balanced fruit. It's extremely delightful—all that delicious fruit flavor—which makes it just perfect to keep everyone from starving as they wait for the food!

Another good bet from Australia is the good-value Angus Brut Pinot Noir Chardonnay NV, which has lots of violet-like floral fruit. This tastes very good with marinated or herb-infused meat, or with fish. If you fancy some pink fizz, how about trying Lindauer Brut Rosé NV, tangy with lots of black cherry flavors? Latecomers don't have to miss out on a glass either, as this New Zealand fizz is good with barbecued fish such as salmon,

as well as with vegetable kabobs or tangy marinated chicken wings and drumsticks.

Certain cavas seem to have the right amount of almost smoky fruit themselves to complement barbecued food, and are particularly delicious with garlicky foods. I can highly recommend the Castell 1909 Cava NV with barbecued chicken and trout, or with anything served in a sweet and sour barbecue sauce.

For more barbecue fizz suggestions, see pages 8 and 61

picnics

Whether you are planning a lazy late picnic lunch or are off with a crowd on one of those pick-and-mix affairs where everyone brings what they want, a medium-bodied fizz is the perfect choice to keep everyone buzzing. One of my favorite champagnes

> The Californian
> fizz, Domaine
> Carneros NV, offers
> a wonderful
> summertime glass
> of red-fruit
> creamy fizz.

for taking to picnics is the Jacquart Brut Mosaïque NV, which has lots of elegant raspberry and violetlike fruit flavors on the palate. It always evokes for me the taste of fresh summer berries, and therefore seems a good suggestion for picnics or indeed any outdoor entertaining. A grape variety that always makes me think of summer is Chenin Blanc, used to make Vouvray in the Loire Valley. It has a slightly honeyed aroma and is heavily perfumed. One of my favorite Vouvrays is the Marc Brédif Brut, which I would thoroughly recommend. Another excellent picnic bubbly is the Californian fizz, Domaine Carneros NV, which offers a wonderful summertime glass of red-fruit creamy fizz.

In England, open-air concerts ending with fireworks have become increasingly popular. At one wonderful concert I went to with friends at Highclere Castle in Berkshire, we enjoyed an amazing picnic supper of salmon, quails' eggs, and lobster, washed down with magnums of chilled Champagne Heidsieck Monopole NV (see also aperitif-style fizzes, pages 54–67). Even the light shower of rain didn't spoil the dry tangy fruit and the subtle, quite rich lemon-meringue flavors on the finish of this fabulous fizz. To give your picnic a touch of style, pack some bottles of Champagne Mumm de Cramant Grand Cru NV. Made from 100% Chardonnay grapes, this has a lovely toasted aroma and hints of buttery, slightly smoky fruit. Try it and discover how well it partners every-thing from shrimp to spicy sausages.

But, more often than not, you're there for the fun, the music, and the party atmosphere— the fizz is the added bonus.

Dare to be different and pour pink fizz, such as the California Korbel Brut Rosé NV, with its delicious raspberrylike aroma and flavor.

The easy-drinking, good-value Seaview Brut NV is another winner for a picnic, while for a really refreshing pink fizz, I'd serve Lindauer Brut Rosé NV. It's a great bargain, with a tangy black-cherry flavor, and you can happily drink it with anything. Whatever you choose, make sure your fizz is well chilled before you set out. It might not look very elegant, but wrapping cold bottles in newspaper will keep the fizz perfectly cool. You can of course use one of the more glamorous champagne cooler-sleeves that fit snugly around the bottle.

For more picnic fizzes, see page 65

supper parties

For those occasions when you are having a relaxed supper, a medium-bodied bubbly is often the best choice. No one's in a hurry; there's plenty of time before sitting down to eat to savor a glass or two of fruity, easy-drinking fizz such as the S. Anderson Napa Valley Brut NV. Dare to be different and pour pink fizz, such as the Korbel Brut Rosé NV, with its delicious raspberrylike aroma and flavor. If you fancy continuing with the fizz throughout the meal, a rosé can be a good bet, especially if you are eating roast lamb, pork, or chicken, or fish. Champagne Louis Roederer Brut Rosé NV is very pale pink, with a light, elegant,

tangy fruit flavor and an aftertaste to die for—raspberries and cream. I've enjoyed both rosés with new-season English roast lamb and redcurrant jelly. The red-fruit flavors in the fizzes seem to accentuate the sweetness of the jelly.

Even the simplest suppers suddenly become more exciting with an accompanying glass of fizz. Korbel Brut NV, for example, goes surprisingly well with hamburgers—its crisp acidity neatly cutting through the richness of the dish. A plate of cold salmon with hollandaise sauce is magically transformed by the relatively rich champagne Billecart-Salmon Rosé NV. Its sister white fizz, Billecart-Salmon Brut Réserve NV, makes a regular appearance in my house. It's the wonderful balance of lightly toasted fruit and elegance that makes this fizz so sexy. Try it with fish dishes and cream sauces; it's sensational. Joseph Perrier Cuvée Royale NV is another favorite champagne of mine. It's a sort of gentle apple-pielike fizz that is elegant yet flavorsome enough to complement a whole range of starters, from artichokes and asparagus (both supposedly difficult to match with wine) to pan-fried scallops.

For more supper-party fizz suggestions, see pages 61 and 76

All the best parties I have ever been to revolved around fizz.
There is simply nothing like getting high on champagne, and

what you'll notice at fizz-only parties is that the bubble doesn't seem to burst—everyone remains on a high all evening.

weddings

Fabulous fizz is an absolute must, whether for a family affair or a grand, formal reception. Guests will be more than delighted with a fruity, easy-drinking yet stylish fizz. There are lots of favorite champagnes that I can recommend. Moët & Chandon NV always shows well, with its creamy nose and almost sweet applelike flavor. Billecart-Salmon Brut Réserve NV has always been one of my favorite wedding champagnes. Another good fizz to drink throughout a wedding reception is the toasty Gosset Brut Excellence NV. Its very tangy fruit flavor always makes it a most welcome and lively choice.

Wedding fizz does not have to be expensive. A very evocative style of wedding fizz for a warm summer's day is the gently honeyed, perfumed Brut Vouvray from Marc Brédif. Yalumba Cuvée One Pinot Noir Chardonnay NV is a deliciously stylish fizz from Australia, with tempting raspberry and vanilla flavors. Should you wish to add a splash of color to this very special event and offer Kir Royale (see page 109) too, those soft summer-fruit flavors are a perfect foil for the cassis. Just as impressive is the Californian Domaine Carneros NV; its creamy texture is a real treat. I often think a sparkling rosé makes a fabulous wedding fizz, especially one as stylish as the strawberry-flavored Etoile Rosé NV, from California's Domaine Chandon. When it comes to a toast for the newlyweds, the question of what to offer is easily solved—bring out a vintage fizz and keep the bubbles rising... (see pages 80–95).

For more wedding fizz suggestions, see pages 10, 65, 72, and 86

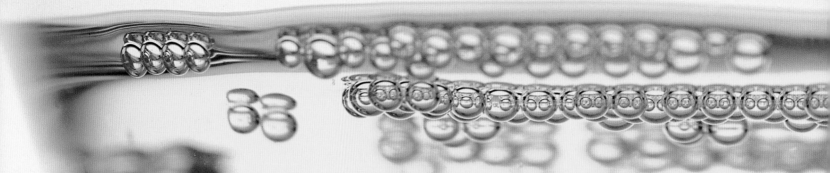

taste notes

A quick reference guide to the best medium–bodied fizzes

France—Champagne

Billecart-Salmon Brut Réserve NV *"Subtle, complex, with creamy vanilla flavors"*

Georges Gardet Cuvée Flavy NV *"Yeasty, with lots of tangy fruit"*

Gosset Brut Excellence NV *"Toasted aroma and tangy fruit"*

Gosset Grande Réserve NV *"Apricots and peaches with a tropical-fruit finish"*

Jacquart Brut Mosaïque NV *"Elegant, with raspberry and violet fruit"*

Joseph Perrier Cuvée Royale NV *"Elegant, apple-pielike champagne"*

Moët & Chandon NV *"Creamy, with a hint of sweet apples"*

Mumm Cordon Rouge NV *"Ice-cream-soda champagne"*

Mumm de Cramant Grand Cru NV *"Elegant, with a toasty, buttery flavor"*

Perrier-Jouët NV *"Tangy fizz with light vanilla on the finish"*

Piper Heidsieck NV *"Honeyed, with creamy caramellike fruit"*

Veuve Clicquot Yellow Label NV *"Stylish, creamy fizz"*

France—Rosé Champagne

Billecart-Salmon Rosé NV *"Delicate, with strawberries-and-cream flavors"*

Louis Roederer Brut Rosé NV *"Light, elegant raspberries-and-cream rosé"*

France—Loire

Marc Brédif Brut Vouvray *"Subtly perfumed with honeyed flavors"*

California

Domaine Carneros NV *"Delicious red fruit creamy fizz"*

Korbel Brut NV *"Easy-drinking fizz with spicy apricot and sherbet overtones"*

S. Anderson Napa Valley Brut NV *"Lemon-sherbetlike, with hints of pear"*

California—Rosé

Gloria Ferrer Blanc de Noirs NV *"Very pale pink with red-fruit flavors"*

Domaine Carneros Rosé NV *"Delicious raspberry-ripple-flavored fizz"*

Domaine Chandon Etoile Rosé NV *"Stylish, strawberrylike fizz"*

Korbel Brut Rosé NV *"Elegant fizz with masses of mouthwatering raspberry fruit"*

Australia

Angus Brut Pinot Noir Chardonnay NV *"Floral, with violetlike fruit"*

Seaview Brut NV *"Smoky aroma, creamy palate, good value"*

Yaldara Reserve Brut NV *"Light, appley, elderflower party fizz"*

alumba Cuvée One Pinot Noir Chardonnay NV *"Complex, with raspberry and vanilla flavors"*

Australia—Rosé

Angus Brut Rosé NV *"Great everyday easy-drinking pink fizz"*

New Zealand

Lindauer Special Reserve NV *"Unusual, yeasty, biscuity, creamy fizz"*

New Zealand—Rosé

Lindauer Brut Rosé NV *"Black-cherrylike tangy fruit"*

Spain

Castell 1909 Cava NV *"White chocolate aroma with tangy licorice and cream on the finish"*

South Africa

abriere Estate Pierre Jourdan Cuvée Belle Rose NV *"Softly fruity, with good balancing acidity"*

the ultimate aperitif

Light-bodied and elegant, crisp and appley, subtle in flavor, ideal for drinking on their own or as an aperitif with food.

fizz is an exhilarating drink; being greeted with a welcome glass of sparkling wine can magically transform the mood into one of celebration. To achieve this sparkling sensation calls for what I describe as the "aperitif-style" fizz. If you like your fizz subtle, this style is for you. Light and elegant, these bubblies taste sensational on their own, work wonders at breaking the ice and making introductions at parties, and will get everyone fizzing.

The great thing about serving a fizz as an aperitif is that you don't have to mess around with hard liqours, mixers, ice, or lemon. All you need are some decent glasses (see pages 134–137) and well-chilled wine. I find that fizz poured from magnums always makes an impressive aperitif.

There's a whole host of fizzes in this section to suit all pockets and preferences—I guarantee you'll discover some wonderful wines to share with your friends (or keep for yourself...). While many of these aperitif-style fizzes are wonderful on their own, they often have enough "weight" of fruit to be equally fabulous with lighter foods. I've suggested occasions where you might enjoy a glass of sparkling wine in isolated splendor—perhaps at the bar while you wait for your friends to arrive—and times when you can happily drink these subtle fizzes with all kinds of delicious food.

bars and restaurants

Waiting for the rest of the crowd to gather, or enjoying a quiet drink before moving on to a restaurant for supper? In anticipation of a good evening, I'd go for a glass of refreshing fizz every time. One of the great things about the bar and restaurant scene now is the increasingly wide range of fizzes you can choose by the glass. Look out for Lindauer Brut NV; this is consistently good and, with its unusual hint of melons and its dry, crisply fruity character, is bound to revive your tastebuds! Cuvée Napa by Mumm Brut NV, with its apple-sherbet aroma and flavor, makes a great alternative. But if you fancy the real thing—and why not?—then Champagne Heidsieck Monopole NV is the one. Light, elegant, and appley, a glass or two of this gentle fizz always goes down extremely well.

For more bar and restaurant fizz suggestions, see page 34

taking a bottle

A good bottle of fizz is the ideal choice to take around to friends. Whether it's for a dinner party or just popping in for a drink, you can guarantee everyone will appreciate a fizzing aperitif. The light, sherbetlike Champagne Lanson Black Label Brut NV is a foolproof choice; and it slips down well with crunchy crudités and dips. An affordable yet tasty, light aperitif suitable for all palates is the Australian fizz, Yaldara Reserve Brut Rosé NV.

just because...

For those moments when you quite simply fancy some fabulous fizz. The ultimate luxury has to be a deep steaming-hot bath and a glass of foaming fizz. My favorite for sipping in the bath is Pol Roger White Foil NV, one of the finest light champagnes around at the

moment. There's something quite decadent about rosé fizz, too. California's Codorníu Napa Rosé NV, with its delicate aroma and flavor of strawberries and raspberries, always seems to hit the spot.

The choices here are endless and really depend on your mood. For exceptional value for money, I find top cavas from Spain are a good bet and much more pleasant to drink than a nondescript (probably acidic) champagne at the same price. Two mouth-wateringly good examples are Codorníu Cuvée Raventós NV and Freixenet Cordón Negro NV (both come in distinctive bottles, too). The easy-drinking Raventós is light, yet complex, with a

creamy nose and floral, soft fruit, while the black-bottled Cordón Negro has an enticing aroma, apple and sherbetlike fruit, with a hint of apricot and melon on the finish.

Sometimes in the late afternoon, when I'm not sure if I'm in "savory" or "sweet" mode, a chilled glass of an Italian fizz such as the exquisitely fragrant Moscato d'Asti from Marco Negri (see page 103 for more producers) is a wonderful solution. With its hint of sweetness on the finish, this style of fizz makes a delicious thirst-quencher. **For more recommended fizzes for those particular moments, see page 35**

the two of you

Any romantic liaison, or indeed one you hope might develop into an affair to remember, has to involve some fabulous fizz. It is, after all, *the* romantic drink and nothing can beat an elegant flute of bubbly as the aperitif to a special evening. Champagne Pol Roger White Foil NV has to be my first choice. It has a lovely elegant aroma with hints of ginger and cream, a perfect balance with good acidity, and a delicious finish. My tasting notes for this favorite fizz simply read "liquid sex in a bottle." Enough said!

THE SOUND OF THY
EXPLOSIVE CORK,
CHAMPAGNE, HAS, BY SOME
STRANGE WITCHERY, OF A
SUDDEN TAUGHT MEN THE
SWEET MUSIC OF SPEECH.
A MURMUR AS OF A RISING
STORM RUNS ROUND THE
TABLE: BADINAGE COMMENCES,
FLIRTATIONS FLOURISH…
WE MIGHT TELL OF
BREAKFASTS, AND OF
SUPPERS, SUDDENLY
CONVERTED FROM SAHARAS
OF INTOLERABLE DULLNESS
INTO OASES OF SMILES AND
LAUGHTER BY THE
APPEARANCE OF CHAMPAGNE.

Charles Tovey, *Wit, Wisdom and Morals, Distilled from Bacchus*

But don't worry, not every date has to be expensive. Good-value pink bubbly can make quite an impression, too. One of my favorite California sparkling wines is the delicious Cuvée Napa by Mumm Rosé NV. A wonderful pale pink, crisp and floral with lots of easy-drinking fruit, this is a consistently good fizz.

For more romantic fizz suggestions, see pages 35 and 84

lazy lunches

If you've got friends coming for lunch—particularly for a barbecue or the kind of help-yourself-affair that lingers on through the afternoon—get things off to a gentle start by serving a good aperitif fizz. The southern French fizz Blanquette de Limoux, Plan Pujade, with its attractively aromatic flavors, or a lemony, lightly honeyed fizz from the Loire Valley's Saumur region would both be a good bet. Try the gently frothing Bouvet Saumur Brut, which has lots of soft, floral fruit and thirst-quenching crispness.

Gloria Ferrer Sonoma Brut NV, with its attractive hints of apples and herbs, is a fabulous lunchtime aperitif fizz. Lighter-style California fizzes like this one have just the right amount of upfront fruit to cope with food as well as offering a delicious mouthful on their own.

Cava is an ideal choice to get everyone in the mood. A classic aperitif-style fizz that is delicious on its own, it has the distinctive flavors to taste good even with spicy eats like garlic-laced olives. Try Sandora Blanc de Blancs Cava Brut NV, with its elegant, earthy fruit and hint of butter on the finish.

For more lazy lunchtime fizz suggestions, see page 35

all-day parties

Fizz always goes down well at parties, particularly early in the day when you need a lift, yet fancy something gentle. The light, refreshing aperitif-style fizzes are ideal, and the good news is that lots of the less expensive fizzes come into their own here, particularly for making Buck's Fizz. A very good party option is Asti Spumante. Light in style (and lower in alcohol), with soft acidity and that hint of sweetness on the finish, it's ideal for sipping on its own. Next time you throw a small party, treat everyone to an Asti Spumante such as Bruno Giacosa Spumante Classico Extra Brut (see page 103 for more producers).

If you enjoy light, soft fizzes, why not try a Loire Valley sparkling wine made from the Chenin Blanc grape, such as Langlois Crémant de Loire? This soft, honeyed, floral French fizz, with its elderflowerlike finish, is the ideal, gentle aperitif, especially when too much acidity would be a shock to the palate (and stomach). Chenin Blanc is a good complement to all sorts of aperitif foods and tastes especially good with smoked trout pâté on melba toasts, crudités, and mushroom or tomato tartlets.

An aperitif-style cava can be a good bet. One of my favorites is the Rondel Premier Cuvée Brut NV, which is light, tangy, and floral and easy to drink. For those of you who can't leave the peanuts and chips alone, it's worth remembering that these crisp, refreshingly acid fizzes are a good foil for salty nibbles. For a touch of style, the refreshing Champagne Lanson Black Label Brut NV will set the tone for the rest of the party. Or how about a glass of the easy-drinking party champagne, Mercier NV? Another great party fizz is the

Australian Yaldara Reserve Brut NV. If you fancy something pink that isn't as expensive as champagne, you can't go wrong with Australian fizz such as the Seppelt Great Western Brut Rosé NV. This fizz tastes particularly good with fish nibbles such as shrimp, oysters, little fish flans, or miniature smoked salmon quiches.

For more party fizz suggestions, see pages 41 and 71

sunday lunches

Sunday lunch with the family in my house is legendary. It's not really surprising when you consider I have eight brothers and sisters, not to mention a similar number of hangers-on (our irreverent term for the in-laws). With so many fizz fans in the family, we invariably start with a glass of bubbly. Champagne Heidsieck Monopole NV is light, elegant, and appley and always goes down well. For such big gatherings, how about trying one of my favorite California fizzes, Cuvée Napa by Mumm Rosé NV, crisp and floral with red fruit overtones? This has the added advantage of being around half the price of its champagne counterpart. These fizzes taste good with tiny scraps of lightly smoked salmon served on brown bread or crostini, garlic croutons with pesto, and cherry tomatoes with goats' cheese and basil.

supper

For simple relaxed suppers with friends, you can't go wrong with a glass of pick-me-up fizz to begin the evening. The light, easy-drinking Gloria Ferrer Sonoma Brut NV from California is a good bet, as is an Australian fizz such as the appley Yaldara Reserve Brut NV. Another Aussie favorite

is Cockatoo Ridge Brut NV, which has an attractive sherbetlike flavor and good acidity. Either serve these Aussie fizzes on their own or simply add a drop of crème de cassis to make a Kir Royale, an attractively colored, tasty, blackcurrant-flavored, fizzy aperitif (see page 109). A dramatic choice of aperitif and so easy to make, but at least it will look as though you made an effort!

For more relaxed supper fizzes, see page 47

celebratory dinner

A celebration is a reason to treat yourself. Nothing beats a glass of fabulous fizz for making you feel special. If you want some seriously good rosé champagne and can persuade some generous-hearted relative or friend to give you a bottle, nothing is finer than Krug Rosé NV. It is simply exquisite, a deliciously light aperitif-style champagne. Extremely pale in color, it has a wonderful delicate balance of red-fruit flavors. Otherwise, serve flutes of the delicious Pol Roger White Foil NV or the strawberry-fruited R. de Ruinart Brut NV—both elegant, refined, and stylish champagnes.

There are plenty of class acts to choose from outside champagne, too. For a very special occasion, you can do no better than to serve Croser (see also vintage fizzes, pages 80–95). The 1994 vintage is one of Australia's finest fizzes, with really stylish, unusual fruit that reminds me of those tiny purple sweets called parma violets. It makes for a superb aperitif and will certainly ensure the dinner gets off to a bubbly start. South Africa is beginning to yield some really exciting sparkling wines in the classic "champagne" style. Krone Borealis Brut NV, Cap Classique is a fabulous combination of gentle fruit and good acidity, making it an ideal—and unexpected—choice to serve at a special dinner.

I'm only a beer teetotaller, not a champagne teetotaller.

George Bernard Shaw, *Candida*

Delicately pale Champagne Piper Heidsieck Rosé NV—
perfect with shrimp, smoked salmon, or red onion tartlets.

al fresco

All the best outdoor meals—whatever time of day or evening they begin—start off with a glass of fizz. Even if the sun isn't shining, fizz can lighten up the atmosphere. I have wonderful memories of a wet summer's day, thanks to the light, vanilla-sherbet Champagne Canard-Duchêne NV we were drinking! For a change, why not try a Crémant from Alsace, with its floral, almost spicy character and gentle fizz? Dopff "au Moulin" Cuvée Julien NV, Crémant d'Alsace, has lots of perfumed fruit—just right for sipping in the backyard on a warm spring day.

While vines have been planted in England since Roman times, the UK hasn't in the past had a reputation for producing any serious bubblies. That, however, has now changed with the arrival of Nyetimber Blanc de Blancs 1992 (see pages 85 and 95) and Chapel Down Epoch Brut NV. The latter is rather distinctive, with an unusual ginger and elderflowerlike aroma and flavor. You will either love it or hate it. Just one whiff of this fizz reminds me of the smell of summer flowers and freshly cut grass.

For more al fresco fizz suggestions, see pages 42 and 75

weddings

You simply can't have a decent wedding without some really good fizz to greet the thirsty guests. Good champagne is, of course, delicious. Laurent-Perrier is one of my favorite wedding fizzes, dry with a steely, "green apple" aroma. It is a very elegant, stylish fizz, and you will find guests will have no problem at all drinking it as they mingle. Rosé makes an interesting choice of aperitif. The delicately pale Champagne Piper Heidsieck Rosé NV, with its unusual violetlike aroma, would be ideal. It tastes good on its own, but also goes well with light foods, such as Champagne Shrimp (see page 116), smoked salmon, kabobs, and red onion tartlets.

Offering fizz to welcome the guests doesn't have to mean saving up for months. There are lots of good, light-style, affordable bubblies around. Look no farther than the Gloria Ferrer Sonoma Brut NV, or pour a cava such as Codorníu Cuvée Raventós NV. With its distinctive floral flavors, cava is a real crowd-pleasing aperitif-style fizz and ideal with canapés and party nibbles, too.

For more wedding fizz suggestions, see pages 10, 52, 72, and 86

taste notes

A quick reference guide to the best aperitif-style fizzes

Champagne

R. de Ruinart Brut *"Light, elegant strawberry fruit"*

Canard-Duchêne NV *"Subtle, with vanilla and sherbet"*

Heidsieck Monopole NV *"Light, elegant, apple sherbet"*

Mercier NV *"Easy-drinking party fizz"*

Pol Roger White Foil NV *"Elegant, perfectly balanced with hints of ginger and cream"*

Lanson Black Label Brut NV *"Light and sherbetlike"*

Laurent-Perrier NV *"Stylish, crisp, apple-citrus flavors"*

France—Rosé Champagne

Piper Heidsieck Rosé NV *"Unusual, violetlike aroma and flavor"*

Krug Rosé NV *"Very pale color, exquisite red-fruit flavor"*

Rest of France

Langlois Crémant de Loire *"Soft, gentle, floral elderflowerlike fizz"*

Dopff "au Moulin" Cuvée Julien, Crémant d'Alsace *"Light, tangy, perfumed fruit"*

Blanquette de Limoux, Plan Pujade *"Aromatic, with a hint of cream"*

Bouvet Saumur Brut *"Soft, honeyed, floral fruit"*

California

Cuvée Napa by Mumm Brut NV *"Apple-sherbet aroma and flavor"*

Gloria Ferrer Sonoma Brut NV *"Light, easy-drinking, with overtones of apples and herbs"*

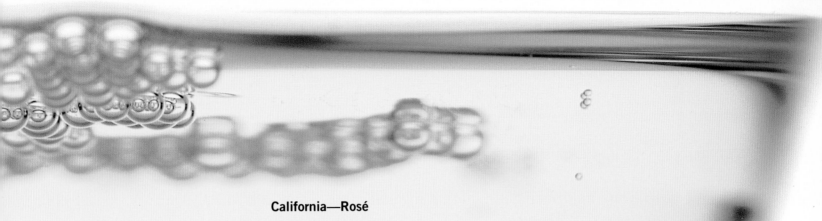

California—Rosé

Cuvée Napa by Mumm Rosé NV *"Crisp and floral with red-fruit overtones"*

Codorníu Napa Rosé NV *"Delicate, with hints of strawberries and raspberries"*

Australia

Yaldara Reserve Brut NV *"Party wine, with appley, elderflower flavor"*

Cockatoo Ridge Brut NV *"Dry, tangy, sherbetlike fizz"*

Australia—Rosé

Yaldara Reserve Brut Rosé NV *"Dry, tangy aperitif"*

Seaview Brut Rosé NV *"Dry and tangy, with lots of red-fruit flavors"*

Seppelt Great Western Brut Rosé NV *"Violetlike nose with mouth-watering, more-ish fruit"*

New Zealand

Lindauer Brut NV *"Unusual hint of melons with a dry, crisp, apple flavor"*

Spain

Codorníu Cuvée Raventós NV *"Complex creamy nose with a floral perfumed aftertaste"*

Freixenet Cordón Negro NV *"Apple-sherbetlike fruit, with a hint of apricot and melon"*

Rondel Premier Cuvée Cava Brut NV *"Tangy fruit flavor and slight caramel on the finish"*

Sandora Blanc de Blancs Cava Brut NV *"Elegant, earthy fruit, with a hint of butter on the finish"*

England

Chapel Down Epoch Brut NV *"Unusual ginger and elderflowerlike aroma and flavor"*

South Africa

Krone Borealis Brut NV, Cap Classique *"Elegant, fresh, and softly fruity"*

fizz with attitude

Full-bodied, creamy, and rich, with plenty of weighty fruit; often with a honeycomb aroma and yeasty character.

fizzes with attitude are for those who like their wines to make a bold statement—rich and full-bodied, with full-on fruit. They are not for the faint-hearted. These are distinctive wines with real character and increased richness that force you to pay attention and savor each mouthful. All of which makes them the ideal choice of fizz for special occasions. If you have a meal planned as part of the celebration, even better, as these fizzes really sparkle with food. They follow on beautifully from the crisp, lighter bubbly you may have had as an aperitif.

Included in this section are some amazing fizzes known as "prestige cuvées" (see also vintage fizzes, pages 80–95). These very special bubblies are made using the finest grapes from the best vineyards. The nonvintage prestige cuvées are a blend of several top vintages—this is the key to achieving consistency and quality of style. Krug Grande Cuvée NV is possibly the epitome of this style of fizz: rich, creamy, it has an almost meaty aroma and exotic aftertaste of vanilla and pears. Wines from as many as ten vintages are blended together to create this fabulous and consistently delicious fizz.

Lovers of pink fizz will find a number of full-bodied rosés that also fit into this richer category. That is one of the joys of fizz—the pleasure in discovering special sparkling wines from around the world that you really enjoy and that you know will add a touch of splendor to any celebratory event.

the ultimate party

For a party that draws attention, make sure you serve a fizz that demands attention. For the truly extravagant among you, Krug Grand Cuvée NV served in magnums is the ultimate party champagne. I doubt you'll find your friends will turn down the offer of a chilled glass of Champagne Bollinger Special Cuvée NV either. This is a big wine, with complex strawberrylike aromas and a long apples, pears, and caramel aftertaste. A glass of this on its own is very, very good. For a stylish champagne that is brilliant value for money (and thus perfect for big parties), offer Champagne Georges Gardet Brut Spécial NV. It's rich, with quite creamy fruit and lots of red-berry flavors; and it always receives rave reviews.

Of course it doesn't have to be champagne to be a fabulous party fizz. There are plenty of affordable sparkling wines with the richness, class and style for any fashion-conscious party. Deutz Marlborough Cuvée NV from New Zealand is great value. Zippy and invigorating, with an unusual honeycomb aroma and lots of creamy fruit, this makes a sensational party fizz. Or how about trying the Spanish Raimat Grand Brut NV, which is a stunning food fizz? This cava has tiny bubbles with an attractive, rich, almost sweet aroma and rich, creamy fruit on the palate. It's a stylish

Zippy and invigorating, with an unusual honeycomb aroma and lots of creamy fruit, Deutz Marlborough Cuvée makes a sensational party fizz.

partner to fresh crab, and fabulous with the Champagne Shrimp (see page 116) and rich white fish dishes.

One of my star fizzes in the massive tasting I did for this book is a wine I hadn't previously tasted, Codorníu Napa Brut NV. From the Spanish cava producer's California winery, it's rich and intense, with masses of raspberry and vanilla ice-cream flavors. Besides being an incredible value for the money, this is versatile and complex enough to drink with just about anything, which makes it an ideal party animal.

For more party fizz suggestions, see pages 41 and 61

special dates

I have to confess I've had a long love affair with Krug. I was drinking Krug when I met my husband; it tasted just as amazing when I celebrated with a glass ten minutes after the birth of my third son Felix. Krug Grande Cuvée NV is the ultimate celebration fizz, definitely worth investing in if you've just fallen in love, passed an exam, pulled off an amazing deal, bought a new house... or simply want to spoil yourself. Expensive, yes, but worth every penny.

Whether it's your birthday or an anniversary, you deserve a glass of fabulous fizz. One of my all-time favorite richer champagnes is Louis Roederer Brut Premier NV, which is complex and creamy with a slightly smoky aroma and well structured, balanced fruit. While this is relatively full-bodied and rich, it also has a wonderful restrained elegance to it. The pleasure with this fizz is that you can savor it on its own and then carry it to the table to enjoy with quite subtle dishes such as ceviche of fish, lightly fried squid, or cucumber mousse.

If you are looking for a distinctive fizz with which to mark a really special occasion, try a bottle of Canard-Duchêne Prestige Cuvée Charles VII NV. Packaged in an unusual, old-fashioned shaped bottle, this is a deliciously rich and creamy champagne with a lingering fruit flavor and a taste of apples and cream on the finish. Nautilus Marlborough Cuvée NV from New Zealand offers a very distinctive "New World" style of toasty, rich and creamy fizz, with lovely fruit, that will make any day a memorable one.

Burgundy for kings, champagne for duchesses, and claret for gentlemen.

French proverb

I suppose the obvious celebration at which to bring out richer fizzes is the wedding meal—be it brunch, lunch, or dinner. I'm all in favor of drinking fizz right through the reception, and simply moving on from the lighter, aperitif-style fizz to these bigger, richer wines during the meal. Domaine Chandon's Cuvée 2000 NV, from the California arm of champagne house Moët & Chandon, is a perfect choice. It's rich, creamy, and elegant, and a perfect partner to dishes such as turbot with a vanilla cream sauce. If you prefer a red meat dish, then Korbel Blanc de Noirs NV may be the answer —certainly an unusual combination but a memorable one, which is what it's all about.

For more celebratory fizz suggestions, see pages 10, 51, 65, and 84

a very special evening

For these occasions fizz is the magical answer. Be it on the deck for a late supper, dining on the terrace at your favorite restaurant and watching the sun go down, or picnicking at a grand open-air concert, why not make an occasion of it and enjoy some fabulous fizz? This is where the richer styles of fizz really come into their own, as they have the weight and fruit to shine through all kinds of foods—spicy or creamy, meat or fish, savory or sweet.

My first choice would be Champagne Charles Heidsieck Brut Réserve NV. It's a very good food wine, with its rich honeycomb aroma and its almost sweet brioche flavor. If you look carefully at the neck label, you'll see the words *"Mis en Cave 1993"* which means the bottle was laid down in the company's cellars in 1993. This new style of labeling tells you how much bottle age your nonvintage champagne has had—generally the longer the bottle age, the richer the wine (see page 129 on how to lay down fizz). Another fizz with that wonderful honeycomb character is the stylish Korbel Chardonnay NV from California. Rich and buttery, this tastes great with spicy, creamy chicken dishes and will happily stay the pace of any outdoor event, grand or intimate.

For more special fizz suggestions, see page 42 and 58

summer lunches

One of the many great things about fizz is that you can choose your fizz to match the occasion and even the season. Think summer time. An ideal Californian fizz for glorious summer days is Mumm Napa Valley Blanc de Blancs NV. Made entirely from Chardonnay grapes, this wine at first appears light and elegant, but has weighty rich, buttery fruit on the palate and aftertaste. This is fabulous on its own, and with creamy chicken or pasta dishes, turbot, or chargrilled or oven-roasted bell peppers. Another fizz I'd recommend is Spain's Raimat Grand Brut NV. Rich in flavor and texture, it retains the classic cava acidity and bite that make it simply perfect as a refreshing yet impressive lunchtime fizz.

Some types of smoked fish such as salmon, trout, or even mackerel can obliterate the flavor of many lighter fizzes. But you'll find richer fizzes will be perfect. Champagne Joseph Perrier Blanc de Blancs Brut NV has an enticing buttery nose, with balanced rich, creamy flavors. This tastes excellent with smoked mackerel pâté served with horseradish sauce. If you are fond of pink fizz, why not try the rich champagne Canard-Duchêne Rosé NV, which has lots of mouth-watering red-fruit flavors? As well as tasting good

with salmon, turbot, and lamb, this fizz is delicious served with any red fruit or tangy summer-fruit dessert.

For more summer fizz suggestions, see page 65

winter dining

Your first reaction might be to reach for a big, flavorsome red wine. But for a special dinner, think again. Have you ever tried fizz with coq au vin? Even though this dish is cooked using red wine, a rich, full-bodied fizz can still shine. Nautilus Marlborough Cuvée NV from New Zealand has just the right amount of toasted, rich, and creamy fruit on the finish to complement this dish. Champagne Deutz Brut Classic NV has a wonderfully intense aroma with an almost meaty, yeasty flavor that makes the perfect partner for poultry; it tastes really good served with roast chicken, cornish hen,

and guinea fowl. So, too, does the deliciously rich, biscuity Domaine Carneros Etoile NV from California.

Again, don't forget the pink fizz. Champagne Gosset Grand Rosé NV is a real showstopper, rich and concentrated, almost sweet on the nose, with ripe red-fruit flavors. Such is the staying power of this fizz, that you can successfully serve it with Thai spicy fish soup, Singapore noodles, and many other oriental dishes that sometimes tax their wine partners. For a combination that will make the evening truly memorable, try this: Champagne Taittinger Prestige Rosé NV with juicy pink roast beef, lightly grilled calves liver, or roast lamb with rosemary. This pink fizz is rich, full-bodied, with lots of upfront fruit flavor, and definitely powerful enough to serve in such company.

For more dinner-party fizzes suggestions, see pages 47, 63, and 87

taste notes

A quick reference guide to the best full-bodied fizzes

Champagne

Bollinger Spécial Cuvée NV *"Rich, complex, with apple, caramel, and cream flavors"*

Canard-Duchêne Prestige Cuvée Charles VII NV *"Apples and cream fizz"*

Charles Heidsieck Brut Réserve, Mis en Cave 1993 *"Honeycomb aroma and flavor, rich, with a hint of sweetness"*

Deutz Brut Classic NV *"Full-bodied, with intense yeasty fruit and flavor"*

Georges Gardet Brut Special NV *"Creamy with the flavor of red berries"*

Joseph Perrier Blanc de Blancs Brut NV *"Complex, with buttery, creamy nuances"*

Krug Grande Cuvée NV *"Complex, with creamy vanilla fruit and hints of apples and pears"*

Louis Roederer Brut Premier NV *"Smoky, rich, complex and restrained"*

France—Rosé Champagne

Canard-Duchêne Rosé NV *"Caramel aromas, with mouthwatering red-fruit flavors"*

Gosset Grand Rosé NV *"Rich and concentrated, with strawberry aromas and flavors"*

Taittinger Prestige Rosé NV *"Tangy and full-bodied, with redcurrant flavors"*

California

Codorníu Napa Brut NV *"Raspberry and vanilla-ice-cream flavors"*

Mumm Napa Valley Blanc de Blancs NV *"Complex, with rich buttery fruit"*

Domaine Carneros Etoile NV *"deliciously rich and biscuity"*

Domaine Chandon Cuvée 2000 NV, Late Disgorged *"Rich and creamy honeycomblike fizz"*

Korbel Chardonnay NV *"Rich and buttery, with honeycomb aftertaste"*

California—Rosé

Korbel Blanc de Noirs NV *"Intense red fruit flavors reminiscent of summer fruit"*

New Zealand

Deutz Marlborough Cuvée NV *"Honeycomb aroma and sherbet, creamylike fruit"*

Nautilus Marlborough Cuvée NV *"Toasted, rich, and creamy fruit"*

Spain

Raimat Grand Brut NV *"Fine mousse with rich, creamy fruit"*

heady stuff

Vintage fizzes, ranging from light to full-bodied; elegant and complex, with intense fruit flavors, sometimes yeasty and biscuity, sometimes with spicy or nutty characteristics.

Vintage fizz is a luxury. Served at all the best events, it's the most stylish, elegant, and romantic of fizzes you can drink. Certain vintage-dated prestige cuvées from the top champagne houses have become legendary. Just think of names such as Moët & Chandon Dom Pérignon, Roederer Cristal, Veuve Clicquot La Grande Dame, and Pol Roger Sir Winston Churchill—names you hear whispered in songs and ordered by stars in Hollywood movies.

Vintage bubblies are made from the finest grapes available in a single year. In good years, when the weather is kind, that fruit can be absolutely stunning; it would be sacrilege to blend it. In other years the outcome can be less good. It's all in the lap of the gods, which somehow makes vintage fizz that much more magical and so very special.

Unless you are horribly rich (and have the luxury to drink it all the time), vintage fizz, especially champagne, is the drink to dream of for those really special occasions. Happily, I have discovered some fabulous vintage fizzes that swiftly drown any guilt about my bank balance. California and Australia make some brilliant value vintage bubblies. So, no debate. Vintage fizz it is to celebrate that lifetime's achievement, a 21st birthday, a special wedding anniversary, a toast to the New Year...

On being asked when she liked to drink her product, Madame Bollinger replied:
"I drink it when I'm happy and when I'm sad. Sometimes I drink it when I'm alone. When I have company, I consider it obligatory. I trifle with it if I'm not hungry and drink it when I am. Otherwise, I never touch it— unless I'm thirsty."

just the two of you

For the truly romantic, no drink can compare to the pleasure of sharing a bottle of vintage fizz. For a stunningly elegant choice of champagne, try Perrier-Jouët Cuvée Belle Epoque, in its strikingly designed art nouveau bottle. The 1990 vintage has an intensely perfumed aroma and flavor of violets and red fruits. This is a superbly fine champagne, and the empty bottle makes an attractive memento of "that moment." Champagne Moët & Chandon Dom Pérignon 1990 is an extremely seductive fizz, which makes it the perfect choice to share with someone very special. Rich yet elegant, with its incredibly complex, yeasty, breadlike aroma and the layers of fruit and whisper of roses on the finish, this has to rate as a "drink in the bath or bed" fizz.

A dreamy California fizz to share with your partner is the aptly named Le Rêve 1992, from Domaine Carneros. Its enticing toasted aroma and flavor, and rich, creamy finish make this the perfect late-night bubbly. Just as with many prestige champagnes, some vintage fizzes from around the world are made in only small quantities and tend to be snapped up. So if a bottle of the light, yet ripe, elegant fizz that is Pelorus 1993—New Zealand's top bubbly from the renowned Cloudy Bay winery—comes your way,

my advice is to keep it to share with your favorite person. The same is true of Oregon's finest fizz, Argyle 1993, a really exotic sparkling wine, with licorice aromas and mouth-watering flavors of strawberries and cream.

For more romantic fizz suggestions, see pages 35 and 58

celebrations

Special "milestone" birthdays, anniversaries, christenings even, demand vintage fizz. Taittinger Comtes de Champagnes Blanc de Blancs 1989 is a wonderful champagne, with a rich biscuity creaminess, yet intensely elegant. Joseph Perrier 1990 Cuvée Royale is an ideal anniversary fizz for those who enjoy full-bodied champagnes; this is rich, with an almost meaty aroma and lots of intense fruit. If you're a fan of big wines, Gloria Ferrer's Carneros Cuvée 1990 is a really sensational vintage California fizz, with a creamy, vanilla, and honeycomb flavor.

For a truly fabulous fizz that will guarantee the celebration gets off to a bubbly start, I'd choose Australia's Croser 1994, an elegant, refreshing fizz with unusual violetlike fruit flavors. Another light, elegant fizz from Down Under is Yalumba Cuvée D 1995, with tangy sherbetlike fruit that provides a wonderfully enlivening mouthful.

Or you could try Seaview Edwards & Chaffey Pinot Noir Chardonnay 1993, which has an amazing vanilla and cream aroma with a honeycomb fruit flavor. This deliciously rich fizz could quite easily be mistaken for a much more expensive champagne.

One of the finest vintage fizzes I've recently tasted was a real surprise, and possibly a cause for celebration in itself! Nyetimber Blanc de Blancs 1992, made in Britain, is simply astonishing—incredibly complex, with masses of buttery, creamy fruit. Even Queen Elizabeth II gave it the royal seal of approval by serving it at her Golden Wedding Anniversary lunch in London. (I should perhaps add that two charming Americans, Stuart and Stanley Moss, make this English fizz.)

For more birthday and anniversary fizz suggestions, see page 72

new year's eve

Some occasions simply don't sparkle without fizz. New Year's Eve is one of them. For a future New Year's Eve party I have laid down some magnums of one of the most sumptuous champagnes, Pol Roger Cuvée Sir Winston Churchill 1988. This deluxe cuvée is named after the wartime British Prime Minister, who was extremely partial to Pol Roger. The 1988 vintage is simply stunning, with perfectly balanced apple-sherbetlike fruit and an aftertaste that carries on long after the wine is finished. This is one to linger over and savor on its own; that said it has the structure to complement seafood and other richly flavored dishes.

I've also laid down one bottle of the rare, covetable Krug Clos du Mésnil 1979, which I shall keep for the chimes at midnight. I was invited to an amazing tasting at the Dorchester Hotel in London in 1998 to celebrate the 300th anniversary of the Clos du Mésnil vineyard. I felt as if I had died and gone to heaven: a tasting of Krug Clos du Mésnil hosted by the man himself, Henri Krug. The 1979 vintage was stunning and has an exotic aroma of filberts and cream with rich, caramel buttery fruit on the palate. If you can get your hands on any vintages of this single-vineyard champagne, despite the hefty price, you will be sure to see in any New Year with immense style as well as fun.

If you are planning a big party and don't want to take out a mortgage, how about serving something like the Australian fizz, Seppelt Salinger 1992? Light, elegant, and floral, this is an ideal drink-all-night party fizz. The Brits could prove their patriotic nature by toasting the New Year with a bottle of Chapel Down Vintage Brut 1993 (see pages 65 and 95), which has unusual fragrant, honeysuckle and spice aromas and flavors. Or try one of the best Spanish vintage cavas I have recently tasted? The excellent Torre de Galle Cava 1994, made in conjunction with champagne Moët & Chandon, is floral in character, with a light,

fruity tang and so easy to drink—a perfect party fizz. So, too, is the California bubbly Iron Horse Sonoma-Green Valley Brut 1994, with its delicate spice and white-chocolate flavors. Add a splash of pink to the evening and serve Schramsberg Napa Valley Brut Rosé Cuvée de Pinot 1994, an exotically fruity pink fizz.

For more party fizz suggestions, see pages 10, 41, 61, 71, and 85

wedding toasts

A delicate choice this, for a very special moment. For the toast at my own wedding, we drank Champagne Heidsieck Monopole

Diamant Bleu 1961. That was the year of my birth, and many guests commented that there was something rather special about toasting the bride with a wine of her own age. Rich, still very lively (just like me, of course!), with a creamy, toasted aroma, it was certainly a fine send-off. It partnered the wedding cake nicely, too. The only other champagne I've recently tasted from that year was a magnum of Lanson 1961. It too was still incredibly young and lively with really stylish, balanced fruit. A somewhat younger fizz, but from a stunning vintage, is Champagne Taittinger Comtes de Champagnes Blanc de Blancs 1989.

This is a sensational fizz to serve as the toast; it's very elegant, with a rich, biscuity creaminess, and again is the perfect partner for a rich fruitcake.

But you don't have to choose champagne for the toast. There are some wonderful quality vintage sparklers that will impress the guests and make a sensational entrance in the proceedings. Why not follow the example of the Spanish Royal Family and serve one of Spain's leading cavas, Juvé y Camps Reserva de la Familia Brut 1994? This is mellow, yeasty, and elegant, with a lovely golden color. A fabulous Aussie fizz that I drank recently at a wedding was Penley Pinot Chardonnay 1991. Although rich in style with an almost sweet honeycomb aroma and flavor, we all found this *very* drinkable!

Two special fizzes from California to keep for such a momentous occasion are Gloria Ferrer Royal Cuvée 1990, a yeasty, spicy, apple-flavored fizz, or the rich, creamy Mumm Napa Valley DVX 1994. And how can I resist including Iron Horse Wedding Cuvée 1996? This is a deliciously light, crisp fizz with spicy berry fruit—perfect to toast the bride and groom.

For more wedding fizz suggestions, see pages 10, 51, 65, and 72

dining in style

This is about decadence. Whether I'm holding a candlelit dinner at home, or dining out somewhere grand and expensive, fabulous fizz *has* to be on the menu. Part of the magic of vintage fizz is that you can enjoy a glass as an aperitif and then select a bottle (or two) to serve with the meal. Champagne Veuve Clicquot Vintage Réserve 1990 is like a meal in itself, with a delicious toasted brioche nose, followed by cream, vanilla, and biscuit flavors on the palate. Complex in flavor, this has real class and would complement crab bisque, pan-fried scallops, or monkfish perfectly.

Champagne's for women.
I stick to Claret.

Clive Newcome from *The Newcomers*, by W. M. Thackeray

Champagne Louis Roederer Brut Vintage 1990, another top fizz from the same vintage, is quite restrained by contrast, with tight, elegant, structured fruit and a lingering aftertaste. It is perfect with foie gras or fish terrine. If you love moules marinière, pick Yellowglen Vintage 1995. This classy fizz from Down Under, with its unusual hint of herbs and honey, is simply divine with this dish.

While pondering the menu and deciding what to eat, consider the fizz, too. Fancy chargrilled chicken? Try the impressive Pelorus 1993 from New Zealand, which has lots of tangy fruit flavor and a hint of butter on the finish. Prefer fish? Champagne Mumm Cordon Rouge 1990 has enough richness *and* citruslike tangy acidity to cut through the flavors of many fish dishes. One fizz that flatters both fish and chicken dishes, particularly those with rich creamy sauces, is the sensational Gloria Ferrer Carneros Cuvée 1990. Although it may not be the first drink that springs to mind, certain vintage fizzes even taste good with roast pork. Pol Roger Vintage Brut 1990 is an apples-and-cream champagne, with lingering fruit. It complements perfectly that classic English dish of roast pork and apple sauce. If you are looking for a wine to serve with lamb, try a vintage rosé such as Champagne Veuve Clicquot Rosé Réserve 1989, with its rich, sherbetlike nose and tangy red fruits.

Don't wrinkle your nose in disbelief, but some vintage fizzes will take you through the main course and on to the dessert. In California recently I enjoyed the pink vintage fizz Mumm Napa Valley Blanc de Noirs 1991 with lamb stuffed with apricots and served in an apricot sauce. I continued drinking this delicious fizz with the raspberry sherbet dessert—it was hard to say which was the more delicious course. I've also discovered a really unusual dish to conclude a special evening—strawberries served with freshly ground black pepper. With it I drank the stylish Oregon fizz, Argyle 1993. The combination was amazing. Try it and see!

For more fizzy dinner-party fizz suggestions, see pages 63 and 76

christmas

There are certain days in the year that are special for very personal reasons. For me Christmas Eve is often more of an occasion than Christmas Day itself. I think it's the anticipation of the fun ahead. One of my fondest memories of a particular Christmas Eve revolves

around a magnum of Champagne Veuve Clicquot La Grande Dame 1985 and grilled fresh lobster. Steely, yet elegant, with amazing balance, this is one of the finest champagnes I've ever tasted. I was sharing it with a close girlfriend, and we found the magnum to be just the right size for the two of us!

On Christmas morning, fizz is an essential accompaniment to the opening of presents over a lazy breakfast. I couldn't recommend too highly the current vintage of La Grande Dame, 1990, which has deliciously ripe fruit, with a touch of yeast; again, an immensely elegant fizz. Even the classy, old-fashioned sealed bottle flatters the special occasion. Another seriously

good Christmas Day breakfast fizz is the California star, Shadow Creek Blanc de Noir 1994. With its stylish, delicious, raspberrylike fruit flavors, it tastes brilliant with herby scrambled eggs.

Dare I mention turkey? Why not cap the festivities by indulging in a bottle of vintage fizz with the big meal? Champagne Canard-Duchêne 1990 has just the right amount of yeasty, doughlike fruit and creamy flavors on the finish to complement roast turkey—it will even cope with mashed potatoes. Champagne Jacquart 1990 is a grand fizz, with marshmallow-like aroma and honeyed sherbetlike fruit on the finish. It is a treat with roast turkey served with cranberry sauce.

My extended family traditionally meets up over a weekend near Christmas to exchange presents. Lunch always starts with champagne; last year we decided on Heidsieck Monopole Rosé 1988. Quite a deep-colored pink fizz, it had masses of mouth-watering tangy fruit flavors that complemented perfectly the heavily-flavored smoked salmon and homemade cheese straws. The King family showed its obvious appreciation by the speed at which the bottles were emptied!

For more Christmas fizzes, see page 101 and 104

For more Christmas fizzes, see page 101 and 104

Please note—the vintages specified in this section were current at the time of writing.

One of my fondest memories of Christmas Eve revolves around a magnum of Veuve Clicquot La Grande Dame 1985 and grilled lobster. Steely, yet elegant, with amazing balance, this is one of the finest champagnes I've ever tasted.

IS THAT CHAMPAGNE?
THEN PUT IT DOWN THE DRAIN!
IT'S BOGUS AND IT'S BILIOUS,
IT'S A BANE.
FORTY BOB A BOTTLE! WELL,
IT MAY AMUSE A PEER;
SOME WOULD TAKE TO WATER IF
THE PRICE OF IT WAS DEAR,
BUT WHO'D BUY A BUBBLY IF IT
COST THE SAME AS BEER?
STILL, IF THAT'S CHAMPAGNE
YOU CAN FILL MY GLASS AGAIN.

A. P. Herbert, *Ballads for Broadbrows*

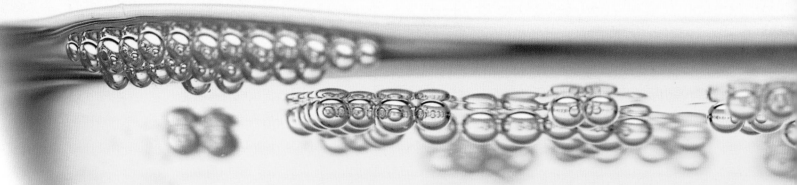

taste notes
A quick reference guide to the best vintage fizzes

France—Champagne

Bollinger Grande Année 1989 *"Stylish with complex white-currant flavors and a hint of lemon butter on the finish"*

Canard-Duchêne 1990 *"Sensational, big yeasty wine with a tasty, tangy finish"*

Moët & Chandon Dom Pérignon 1990 *"Complex, yeasty bready aroma and sensational fruit"*

Dom Ruinart Blanc de Blancs 1988 *"Honey and lemon aroma and flavor, creamy finish"*

Heidsieck Monopole Diamant Bleu 1961 *"Creamy, toasted aroma"*

Jacquart Blanc de Blancs 1992 Cuvée Mosaïque *"Appley fruit with honeyed sherbet finish"*

Jacquart 1990 *"Marshmallow aroma with honeyed sherbet fruit"*

Joseph Perrier 1990 Cuvée Royale *"Full-bodied, with intense concentrated fruit"*

Krug Vintage 1989 *"Rich and intense yet with elegant sherbetlike fruit"*

Krug Clos du Mésnil 1979 *"Filbert characters, with an exotic, buttery, creamy finish"*

Krug Clos du Mésnil 1989 *"Quite restrained, steely fruit yet creamy on the finish"*

Louis Roederer Brut Vintage 1990 *"Elegant, with masses of tangy, complex fruit"*

Moët & Chandon 1992 *"Perfumed, floral, violet aroma and flavor with a light creamy finish"*

Mumm Cordon Rouge 1990 *"Rich, with citruslike tangy sherbet acidity"*

Perrier-Jouët 1990 Cuvée Belle Epoque *"Intensely perfumed aroma and elegant flavor of violets and red fruit"*

Pol Roger Vintage Brut 1990 *"Stylish, apples-and-cream champagne"*

Pol Roger Cuvée Sir Winston Churchill 1988 *"Complex, with lasting apple-sherbet flavor"*

Taittinger Comtes de Champagnes Blanc de Blancs 1989 *"Elegant, with rich, biscuity creaminess"*

Veuve Clicquot Vintage Réserve 1990 *"Toasted brioche nose with cream and vanilla on the pala*

Veuve Clicquot La Grande Dame 1990 *"Complex, deliciously ripe yeasty fruit"*

France—Rosé Champagne

Heidsieck Monopole Rosé 1988 *"Deep color with complex red-fruit flavor"*

Veuve Clicquot Rosé Réserve 1989 *"Stylish red-fruit flavor with sherbet finish"*

Spain

Cava Juvé y Camps Reserva de la Familia Brut 1994 *"Elegant, mellow, and yeasty"*

Torre de Galle Cava 1994 *"Floral, tangy, party fizz"*

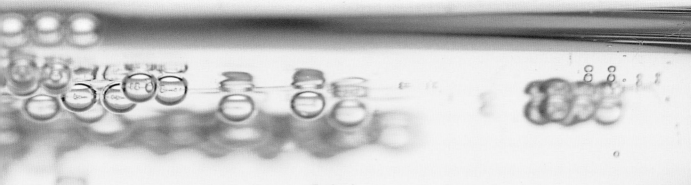

England
Chapel Down Vintage Brut 1993 *"Aromatic honeysuckle and spice fizz"*
Nyetimber Blanc de Blancs 1992 *"Stylish and complex with buttery, creamy fruit"*

Australia
Croser 1994 *"Stylish, unusual, with violetlike refreshing fruit"*
Green Point Brut 1995 *"Toasted aroma and exquisitely balanced fruit"*
Penley Pinot Chardonnay 1991 *"Stylish, honeycomblike fizz"*
Seaview Edwards & Chaffey Pinot Noir Chardonnay 1993 *"Rich, vanilla and cream fizz"*
Seaview Pinot Noir Chardonnay 1995 *"Rich, creamy fizz, good with smoked fish and meat"*
Seppelt Salinger 1992 *"Elegant, floral nose with stylish red-fruit flavor"*
Yalumba Cuvée D 1995 *"Elegant, with rich, zippy, sherbet flavors"*
Yellowglen Vintage 1995 *"Perfumed, honeyed fizz"*

California
Domaine Carneros 1993 *"Rich yet delicate, with lemon-butter nuances"*
Domaine Carneros Le Rêve 1992 *"Toasted aroma and flavor and rich, creamy finish"*
Gloria Ferrer Carneros Cuvée 1990 *"Rich, creamy with vanilla and honeycomb flavors"*
Gloria Ferrer Royal Cuvée 1990 *"Yeasty aromas and spicy apple flavors"*
Iron Horse Sonoma-Green Valley Brut 1994 *"Light, with delicate spice and white-chocolate flavors"*
Iron Horse Wedding Cuvée 1996 *"Exotic light and crisp fizz, with spicy berry fruit"*
Mumm Napa Valley Blanc de Noirs 1991 *"Intense, raspberry-and-vanilla-ice-cream fizz"*
Mumm Napa Valley DVX 1994 *"Rich, creamy fizz with hints of filberts"*
Mumm Napa Valley Vintage Reserve 1994 *"Delicious apple-pie-and-ice-cream fizz"*
Schramsberg 1992, J. Schram *"Elegant, with hints of filberts and stunning, lingering currantlike aftertaste"*
Shadow Creek Blanc de Noir 1994 *"Light with stylish red-fruit flavor"*

California—Rosé
Schramsberg Napa Valley Rosé Cuvée de Pinot 1994 *"Hints of raspberries, peaches, and cinnamon"*

Oregon
Argyle 1993, Willamette Valley *"Stylish, with a yeasty nose and a hint of licorice"*

New Zealand
Deutz Blanc de Blancs 1994 *"Elegant, with a flavor of Ogen melons and sherbet"*
Pelorus 1993 *"Elegant, tangy, fruity fizz"*

demi-sec bubblies

Softly fruity demi-sec fizzes, with a subtle balance of sweetness and refreshing, tangy acidity.

i n the early part of the 20th century, demi-sec champagne was *the* society fizz. All the right people drank it; and it certainly kept the 1920s "roaring." Now with the start of a new century, it seems this style of sweeter fizz is enjoying something of a cult revival, which I think is brilliant, as there are some really exciting, seductive sweet sparkling wines around. Start looking and you will quickly uncover these gently sweet bubblies (look out for the term demi-sec or occasionally *riche*) in stores and on restaurant wine lists.

As you'll discover, "sweet" doesn't necessarily mean heavy, or sugary. The great thing about good-quality demi-sec fizz is that it has a subtle balance of sweetness and refreshing, tangy acidity. It is this "backbone" of acid—a crisp, sherbetlike, tangy taste on the finish—that stops the fizz from tasting cloyingly sweet. On a sweetness scale of 1–9, where 1 indicates a bone-dry wine and 9 a very rich, sticky sweet one, most demi-sec sparkling wines tend to weigh in at around 6. The popular, gently sweet Italian sparkler Asti Spumante (see page 103), for example, averages 7.

Some people say this style of fizz is an acquired taste. What is closer to the truth is that many may simply not have tasted a good-quality demi-sec fizz with the finesse and style of those you'll find here. And they've no doubt not drunk it in the company of the most flattering dishes, because, as with many of the richer fizzes in this book, sweet fizz undoubtedly tastes at its best with food. With dessert it is superb—fruit-based ice creams and sherbets are beautifully complemented by demi-sec fizz.

So dare to be different, join the cult, and offer your guests a glass of gently sweet fizz with their dessert. Just don't be surprised if they ask for a second glass to enjoy on its own afterward. If you know your friends will enjoy the fun of experimenting with unusual combinations, take a look at the fizzes I've suggested here to serve with a main dish; you'll be amazed at the stunning combination they can make. And it's guaranteed to get everyone talking.

desserts

I defy anyone who "thinks" they won't enjoy a sweet fizz not to be seduced by Champagne Louis Roederer Riche NV. The current nonvintage has an intense, toasted, caramelly aroma with a hint of almonds on the palate. While rich, it is not very sweet at all, with just an attractive touch of honey before the refreshing zip of acidity on the finish. Recently I served some half-bottles of aged Louis Roederer Riche (you could tell they were old from the indented corks and the deep color of the wine). They were absolute nectar and slipped down beautifully with the tutti-frutti champagne sherbet that I served, which had crunchy bits of raspberry in it.

Fruit-based desserts and sweet fizzes are really made for each other. You can enjoy a glass of demi-sec with anything from an apple cobbler, a tarte Tatin or caramelized oranges to fruit pudding and strawberry Pavlova. Champagne Pol Roger Demi-Sec NV, with its creamy applelike flavor, tastes amazing with apple pie and cream, or baked apples filled with sultanas and cinnamon. Lots of other desserts make perfect demi-sec partners, too. Try serving an old favorite such as bread and butter pudding with a glass of Champagne Canard-Duchêne Demi-Sec NV, which has an

"A life of pleasure-seeking, card playing and dissipation brings only dissatisfaction. You will find that one day."
"Oh I know it turns out that way sometimes," assented Reginald. "Forbidden fizz is often the sweetest."
But the remark was wasted on the princess, who preferred Champagne that had at least a suggestion of dissolved barley-sugar."

Saki, *Reginald in Russia*

Fruit-based desserts and sweet fizzes are really made for each other. You can enjoy a glass of demi-sec with anything from an apple cobbler, a tarte Tatin or caramelized oranges to fruit pudding and Pavlova.

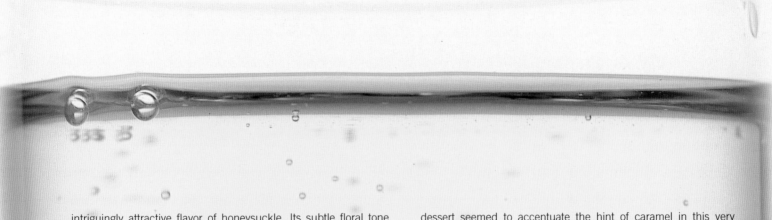

intriguingly attractive flavor of honeysuckle. Its subtle floral tone works exceptionally well with the delicate perfumed flavor of Champagne and Rose-Petal Sherbet (see page 120). I've also enjoyed this fizz with butterscotch ice cream, the flavor of which can sometimes be flattened by still sweet wines.

If you want to win over the most doubting of friends, give them a glass of a refreshingly light, elegant demi-sec fizz such as the sweetly fruity Bouvet Saumur Demi-Sec. With its characteristic honeyed Chenin Blanc character and gently spritzy character, this is a lovely summery style of sweet fizz.

Sadly, chocolate is a bit of a problem. Rich chocolate mousse, for example, can swamp the fizz. However, for those of you who simply love chocolate, I have found a solution or two. A glass of sweet fizz such as the Champagne Piper Heidsieck Demi-Sec NV, with its creamy sherbet flavors and floral finish, will complement a light chocolate dessert. Asti Spumante can withstand a limited chocolate onslaught, too. Or you can be really daring and pour a sparkling red fizz (see page 104).

Asti Spumante is a star choice to serve with a steamed fruit pudding, by the way. As light and gently sweet as the pudding can be dark and heavy, this soft, spritzy Italian fizz really revives the taste buds! (See page 103 for top producers.) While there are not yet that many sweet sparklers made outside Europe, one worth searching for is the Australian Green Point Riche NV. I recently tasted it with a dish of broiled figs served with sour cream and orange caramel. It was a fabulous combination. The caramel in the dessert seemed to accentuate the hint of caramel in this very stylish, again not overtly sweet bubbly. Just as fabulous is Schramsberg Napa Valley Crémant 1995. This is a very easy-to-drink sweet fizz, with a delicious raspberry-ripplelike flavor.

Fashionable desserts such as sticky toffee pudding or pecan pie taste good with demi-sec, too. For a relaxed Friday evening supper, why not indulge in the grapey Asti Spumante or a demi-sec cava from Spain, two really affordable sweet fizzes? One of the nicest cavas that I have recently enjoyed is Rondel Premier Cuvée Demi-Sec NV. It is floral and sweet, yet superbly balanced. Strangely enough, it tastes great with spicy, Asian dishes, too....
For more dessert fizz suggestions, see page 88

nonsweet dishes

Believe it or not, demi-sec fizz can be sensational with nonsweet dishes too. For an unusual, yet very successful pairing, serve it with lobster bisque or fish pâté as an appetizer. It's quite amazing how that touch of sweetness in the wine allows it to stand up to powerful food flavors. This style of fizz is also a good foil for duck, especially in Chinese-style dishes such as Peking duck, where the sweetness complements the richness of the plum sauce. Shrimp or fish, such as monkfish served with garlic and chili, or sea bass cooked Thai-style with lemongrass also, taste especially good with an accompanying glass of demi-sec. Go on, be adventurous, try any of these nonsweet dishes with one of the recommended demi-sec fizzes on pages 102–103.

taste notes
A quick reference guide to the best demi-sec fizzes

France—Champagne

Canard-Duchêne Demi-Sec NV *"Pale gold with honeysuckle sweetness"*

Louis Roederer Riche NV *"Toasted caramel, almondy aroma and flavor"*

Piper Heidsieck Demi-Sec NV *"Creamy, floral, sherbet flavors*

Pol Roger NV Demi-Sec NV *"Apples and cream with sherbet on the finish"*

France—Loire

Bouvet Saumur Demi-Sec *"Fresh and elegant, gently honeyed fizz"*

Spain—Cava

Rondel Premier Cuvée Demi-Sec NV *"Floral, spicy, sweet fizz"*

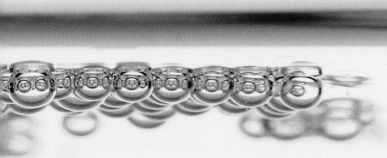

Australia

Green Point Riche NV *"Stylish, with hints of caramel and citrus acidity on the finish"*

California

Schramsberg Napa Valley Crémant 1995 *"More-ish, with a delicious raspberry-ripple flavor"*

Italy—Asti

Asti Spumante—*top producers include Asti Martini, Fontanafredda, and Bruno Giacosa*

Moscato d'Asti—*top producers include Marco Negri, Alasia, La Morandina, La Spinetta,*

Saracco Paolo, Vignaioli di Santo Stefano Belbo

wicked and red

Full-flavored, rich and sweetly fruity red fizzes, with a dry, slightly tannic finish

If you are searching for a really original style of bubbly that will make your friends sit up and take notice, why not try a spectacular red fizz? These are serious but fun sparkling wines. An acquired taste, yes, but if you like them, you'll love them. Just watch people's faces as the cork pops and all that frothing purple fizz comes pouring out. Made from the spicy, plummy Shiraz grape, Australia produces a unique style of fabulous red fizz that is now spreading its influence around the globe. While there aren't yet that many widely available, these unusual fizzes are worth seeking out.

Probably the most fabulous I have tasted to date is Mitchell's extremely full-bodied tannic Peppertree Sparkling Shiraz NV. Richly spicy in aroma and flavor, with a hint of black pepper, this is a classic Aussie sparkling red and a great introduction to the style. An indulgent option is the Seppelt Show Sparkling Shiraz. A vintage-dated fizz, it is allowed to mature for over eight years before release, and is much sweeter, softer, and more approachable because of that bottle age. Its younger brother, Sparkling Shiraz from Seppelt (the current vintage is 1994) has an amazing black-cherry aroma and earthy bitter chocolate flavors. Australia also makes red fizz from the Cabernet Sauvignon grape. Yalumba Cuvée Two Sparkling Cabernet NV has a wonderful aroma of black-currants with a hint of cinnamon spice.

Believe it or not, sparkling reds are fabulous with food, both savory and sweet.

Chilled Sparkling Shiraz is a traditional accompaniment to Christmas turkey and cranberry sauce Down Under. It also works wonders with East Indian dishes; or choose a red fizz with those dark red-fruit and bitter chocolate characters for a wickedly good partner to dark chocolate torte. Try the Yalumba Cuvée Two with a good blue cheese such as English Stilton.

California now boasts some stunning red fizzes made from the seductive Pinot Noir grape variety. And as I discovered on a recent trip, they are quite extraordinarily good served with red meat, such as lamb or beef. Korbel Rouge NV is a full-bodied fizz, with an unusual licorice flavor. Schug Rouge de Noir 1996 positively brims with intense strawberry-jam fruit.

A quick reference guide to the best red fizzes

Australia

Peppertree Sparkling Shiraz NV, Mitchell *"Intense, spicy, with hints of black pepper"*

Seppelt Sparkling Shiraz 1994 *"Black-cherry with bitter chocolate flavors"*

Seppelt Show Sparkling Shiraz 1985 *"Plummy, sweetish fruit with a bitter-sweet finish"*

Yalumba Cuvée Two Sparkling Cabernet NV *"Blackcurrants and cinnamonlike spice"*

California

Korbel Rouge NV *"Full-bodied, spicy, licoricelike red fizz"*

Schug Rouge de Noir 1996 *"Mouth-watering, strawberry-jam fruit"*

Mumm Sparkling Pinot Noir NV *"Delicious aroma and flavor of fraise des bois"*

Kornell Rouge NV *"Floral overtones, with raspberry-ripplelike finish"*

Just watch people's faces as the cork pops and all that frothing purple fizz comes pouring out.

fizz cocktails and recipes

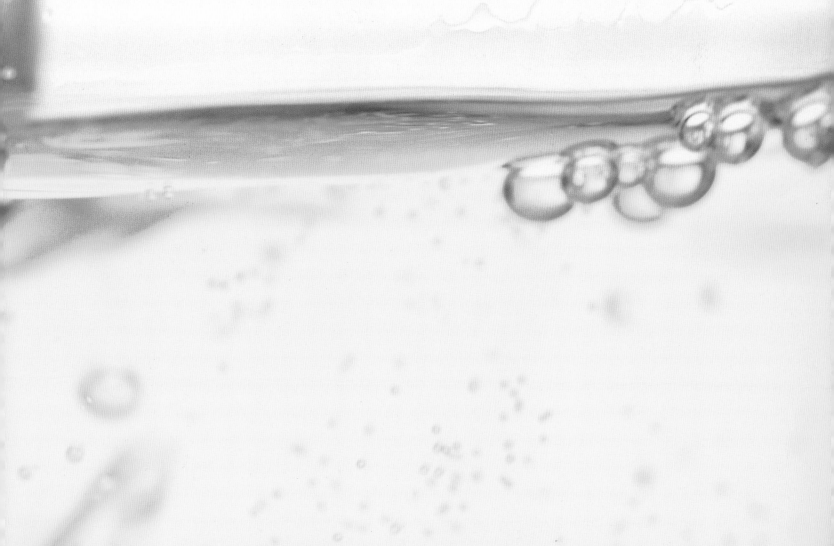

The secret to making successful cocktails at home is to keep them simple. And with fabulous fizz as the main magic ingredient, they are bound to taste good! The million-dollar question is, of course, what sort of fizz should you use? Personally, I think it is a mistake to use vintage, deluxe champagne or the very best, most expensive sparkling wines. Instead I prefer a light- to medium-bodied, everyday kind of fizz, such as the affordable and great-quality Australian Angus Brut NV, the consistently good California fizz Mumm Cuvée Napa NV or Spanish cava, or for something slightly more fruity, a French sparkler such as Blanquette de Limoux. If you want much sweeter cocktails, use a sweet demi-sec fizz or a sweet Italian fizz such as Asti Spumante or Moscato d'Asti.

In terms of quantities, to avoid measuring out ingredients, simply keep to the proportions stated and gauge the measure by eye. This means you can make as much or as little as you wish, irrespective of the size of the glass or pitcher. When making fruit-based cocktails, always use freshly squeezed fruit juice for a more refreshing taste.

Finally, as ever with fabulous fizz, make sure it is thoroughly chilled and don't be tempted to make cocktails in advance or you will reduce the all-important bubble-count.

cocktails

bellini

A classic cocktail that originated in Venice and traditionally is made with puréed white peaches. It's simple yet delicious and one glass inevitably leads to another.

3–4 ripe peaches, skinned, stones
    removed, and flesh cut into chunks
peach brandy (optional)
1 bottle brut fizz

In a blender, whizz the peaches to a purée, then chill. Fill 6–8 champagne flutes one-third full of purée, dash with brandy, if using, and top with chilled fizz.

buck's fizz

Perfect as a toast at a breakfast reception or served as an aperitif. Created by the bartender at Buck's Club, London, in 1921.

1 part freshly squeezed orange juice
Grenadine (optional)
2 parts brut fizz
1 slice of orange (optional)

Pour the orange juice into a champagne flute, dash with Grenadine, if using, and top up with chilled fizz. Add a slice of orange, if using, then serve.

kir royale

Stylish and delicious, with a rich blackcurrant flavor. Vary the liqueur to create another cocktail—use crème de framboise, made from raspberries, or crème de mûres, made from blackberries.

crème de cassis, to taste
1 part brut fizz

Put a few drops, about ½ teaspoon, of crème de cassis into a champagne flute, top up with chilled fizz, and stir to mix.

champagne julep

Excellent for summertime entertaining—outside in the open air or under cover in a party tent. It's suitably light and refreshing.

1 sugar cube
1 part brut fizz
1 sprig of fresh mint

Put a sugar cube into a champagne flute or saucer glass, and top up with chilled sparkling wine. Add a sprig of fresh mint to the glass, then serve.

champagne pick-me-up

The title says it all! Why not enjoy this cocktail while relaxing in a hot bath?

1 part brandy
1 part dry white vermouth, sweet white
    vermouth or sweet red vermouth
superfine sugar, to taste
4 parts brut fizz

Put the brandy, vermouth, and sugar in a champagne flute or saucer glass. Top up with chilled sparkling wine.

blue rinse fizz

A heavenly cocktail—electric-blue in color—with a tropical feel.

4 dashes or 1 teaspoon blue Curaçao
1 part brut fizz
1 slice of orange

Chill a champagne flute in the freezer for 1 hour. Add the Curaçao and swirl it around the glass to coat the inside. Add the fizz and serve with a slice of orange.

champagne st. clements

Refreshingly tangy, the bittersweet flavor of the Cointreau and lime makes this fizzy cocktail mouthwateringly good.

1 part freshly squeezed lemon or lime
    juice
1 part Cointreau
4 parts brut fizz
1 slice of orange, lemon or lime

Mix the lemon or lime juice and Cointreau with some crushed ice, then pour into a tall glass to about one-third full. Top up with chilled sparkling wine and serve with a slice of orange, lemon or lime.

black velvet

Sex in a glass—rich in body with silky smooth bubbles. Created in 1861 at Brook's Club, London. For a match made in heaven, serve this cocktail with oysters— an acclaimed aphrodisiac.

1 part brut fizz
1 part draught stout such as Guinness
    or Murphy's (draught stout is available
    in cans)

Chill the fizz and stout, then pour them simultaneously into a tall glass. To create a very frothy head on the cocktail, add a dash more fizz. For a sweeter cocktail, use Murphy's instead of Guinness.

champagne cocktail

An extremely chic aperitif. The effervescent bubbles spiraling their way to the top as the sugar dissolves is quite hypnotic.

dash of Angostura bitters
1 sugar cube
1 teaspoon brandy or Cognac
1 part brut fizz

Put a sugar cube in a champagne saucer glass and dash with Angostura to soak. Add the brandy and top with chilled fizz.

calypso fizz

One taste will transport you to the exotic shores of the Caribbean!

1 part white rum or coconut rum
1 part banana or orange liqueur, such as Cointreau
dash of Angostura bitters (optional)
4 parts brut fizz
1 slice of banana
1 slice of orange

Put some crushed ice in a champagne saucer glass. Add the rum and the banana or orange liqueur, and dash with Angostura bitters, if using. Top up with fizz and stir gently to mix. Serve with a slice of banana and a twist of orange.

death in the afternoon

Said to be one of Ernest Hemingway's favorites when he lived in Paris.

1 part Pernod
5 parts brut fizz

Pour the Pernod into a champagne flute and add chilled sparkling wine to give a milky opalescent cocktail.

mexican sunrise

Unusual bittersweet flavor. Gold tequila is a must—it is richer, smoother, and sweeter than standard tequila.

4 parts brut fizz
1 part gold tequila
1 part freshly squeezed lemon juice
1 teaspoon clear honey (optional)

Put the chilled fizz, gold tequila, and lemon juice in a tall glass, then stir in the honey, if using. Serve with a straw.

alfonso fizz

Desposed in 1931, Spanish King Alfonso XIII bid a hasty retreat to France, where he made his time bearable with this drink.

1 sugar cube
3 drops Angostura bitters
1 part Dubonnet
4 parts brut fizz
1 slice of lemon

Put the sugar cube in a champagne flute or saucer glass and add the Angostora. Add a large ice cube, the Dubonnet, and chilled fizz. Serve with a twist of lemon.

champagne charlie

Named after the infamous Charles Heidsieck—this is a true party drink.

4 parts Charles Heidsieck NV
1 part apricot brandy
1 slice of orange

Half fill a glass with crushed ice. Add the fizz and brandy. Serve with the orange slice.

champagne fruit punch

Make at the last minute or you will lose the fabulous fizz. If unexpected guests arrive, simply add more fizz or water to replenish the punch.

2 parts sparkling wine, such as Asti
    Spumante or Moscato d'Asti
1 part sparkling mineral water
½ part brandy
⅛ part cherry brandy
freshly squeezed lemon juice, to taste
sugar, to taste
a selection of fruit, such as peach slices,
    cherries, raspberries, orange slices,
    pineapple chunks, starfruit slices, and
    kiwi slices
sprigs of fresh mint, to serve

Put all the ingredients, except the fruit, in a punch bowl or large glass bowl and stir to mix. Add the fruit and mint and serve in tall glasses or champagne flutes.

champagne float

An alcoholic version of the all-time-favorite, ice cream soda.

1 large scoop vanilla ice cream
1 tablespoon cherry brandy
dash of Cointreau (optional)
1 part brut fizz
raspberries, to serve

Put the ice cream in a tall glass. Add the cherry brandy and Cointreau, if using, and top with chilled sparkling wine. Stir gently to mix, then add the raspberries. Serve with a straw and soda spoon.

fizzy applejack

A treat for lovers of apple brandy.

1 part Calvados
dash of Grenadine
4 parts brut fizz
1 slice of apple

Pour the Calvados, Grenadine, and fizz into a glass and serve with a slice of apple.

cherry froth

Seriously potent. You've been warned!

1 part vodka
1 part cherry brandy
dash of freshly squeezed lime juice
2 parts brut fizz
1 fresh cherry

Pour the vodka, brandy, and lime juice
into a tall, long-stemmed glass. Top with
chilled fizz and serve with a cherry.

the holy grail

*Christened appropriately—Benedictine
and Champagne are both thought to have
been invented by monks.*

4 parts brut fizz
1 part brandy
1 part Benedictine
1 part Cointreau
peach or nectarine slices, to taste
1 sprig of fresh rosemary

Mix the first 4 ingredients together, add
the fruit, and serve with a sprig of rosemary.

carribean cruiser

Have a few of these and you'll be floating!

1 part freshly squeezed orange juice
1 part golden rum
dash of lemon juice
3 parts brut fizz
1 sugar cube (optional)

Put the orange juice, golden rum, and
lemon juice in a champagne flute and top
with chilled fizz. Drop in the sugar cube,
if using, then serve.

texas fizz

*Take your time over this intoxicating
cocktail. If it proves too powerful, replace
half of the fizz with tonic water.*

1 part gin
2 parts freshly squeezed orange juice
dash of Grenadine
4 parts brut fizz
1 slice of orange

Put some ice in a large tumbler, then
add the gin, orange juice, and Grenadine.
Top up with chilled fizz and serve with a
twist of orange.

melon bubble
Quite a lethal concoction!

2 parts gin
1 part Midori (melon liqueur)
1 part Poire William
4 parts dry brut fizz (if you prefer
    something sweet and grapey, use
    Asti Spumante)
melon balls or pear slices, to serve

Half fill a champagne flute or saucer glass
with the gin, Midori, and Poire William.
Top up with chilled fizz and serve with
melon balls or pear slices.

citrus toast

*A mouth-tingling, refreshing fizz —use it
for the toast at any celebration.*

1 sugar cube
1 part Grand Marnier
1 part freshly squeezed lime juice
2 parts freshly squeezed orange juice
2 parts brut fizz
slices of lime or small oranges, to serve

Put the sugar cube in the bottom of a
champagne flute or saucer glass. Add
the remaining ingredients and serve with
slices of lime or orange.

cooking with fizz

Marvelous to drink and wonderful to cook with—fizz imparts a subtle, light flavor that complements fish and seafood, chicken, wild mushrooms and delicate fruits such as peaches, cherries, and most berries. Don't use expensive bubblies; instead opt for a value-for-money fizz such as Spanish cava, Australian fizzes like Angus Brut NV or Seaview NV, New Zealand Lindauer Brut NV or the California brut fizz, Mumm Cuvée Napa NV.

champagne shrimp

Fizz enhances the delicate flavor of seafood perfectly. A wonderful dinner-party starter or a special light-lunch treat.

4 tablespoons sweet butter

12 small shallots, halved

36 large uncooked shrimp, shelled and deveined, tail fins left on

2 tablespoons brandy, warmed

1 cup fizz, such as New Zealand Lindauer Brut NV

1 cup crème fraîche

sea salt and freshly ground black pepper

sprigs of fresh dill or chervil, to serve

Italian ciabatta bread, to serve

Serves 6 as a starter or 3 as a main course

Heat the butter in a wide skillet, add the shallots and sauté gently until softened but not browned, about 3–5 minutes. Add the shrimp and cook until opaque—about 3 minutes, but no longer or they will be tough. Remove the shrimp and shallots with a slotted spoon and reserve. Pour the warmed brandy into the skillet, light with a match and let the alcohol burn off. Add the fizz and bring to a boil, then reduce the heat and simmer until the liquid has reduced by half. Stir in the crème fraîche and add the salt and freshly ground black pepper. Cook the sauce for 2 minutes. Reduce the heat and return the shrimps and shallots to the skillet to heat through. Serve with sprigs of fresh dill or chervil and crusty bread, such as ciabatta, to mop up the juices.

champagne chicken

Succulent and tender with a subtle tang and richness from the fizz. Elegant simplicity is the key to this superb dish.

2 tablespoons butter
1 teaspoon peanut or corn oil
6 slices pancetta or 4 slices smoked
    streaky bacon, cut in strips
1 chicken, cut into 8 pieces
¼ bottle brut fizz, such as Mumm
    Cuvée Napa NV
2 sprigs of fresh tarragon, chopped, plus
    extra to serve
sea salt and freshly ground black pepper
Serves 6-8

Heat the butter and oil in a large skillet. Add the pancetta or bacon and fry until crispy, then remove and drain on paper towels. Add the chicken pieces to the skillet and cook for 5 minutes on each side until golden. Pour in the fizz, bring to a boil and let bubble for 1–2 minutes. Add the crispy pancetta or bacon and tarragon. Bring back to a boil, cover, and reduce to a gentle simmer. Cook the chicken until tender, about 50 minutes, basting 2–3 times during cooking. (If the sauce reduces too much, add a few tablespoons of water or chicken stock) Serve with sprigs of tarragon, boiled new potatoes, and sautéed mushrooms.

wild mushroom and champagne risotto

A remarkable risotto. For best results, use the finest and freshest ingredients, and whatever wild mushrooms are in season.

½ oz. dried porcini mushrooms
8 oz. assorted fresh wild mushrooms,
    such as oyster, chanterelle, morel, and
    shiitake, or button mushrooms
6 tablespoons sweet butter
1 tablespoon olive oil
1 onion, finely chopped
1 garlic clove, crushed
2½ cups Italian risotto rice
1 large glass fizz, such as Angus Brut NV
6 cups chicken or vegetable stock, kept
    simmering
sea salt and freshly ground black pepper
chopped flat-leaf parsley, to serve
Serves 4 as a light lunch or 6 as a starter

Put the dried porcini in a small bowl, cover with hot water, and let soak for 10 minutes. Strain through a cheesecloth-lined strainer and reserve the soaking liquid, then coarsely chop the porcini mushrooms. Using a damp cloth, wipe clean the fresh mushrooms (do not wash the mushrooms) and thickly slice any that are large.

Heat 2 tablespoons of the butter and the oil in a large saucepan. Add the onion and cook until softened but not browned, about 5 minutes, then add the garlic and cook for 2 minutes more. Add the fresh wild mushrooms, fry gently for 2 minutes, then add the chopped porcini.

Add the rice and stir until the grains are translucent. Pour in the fizz and the reserved soaking liquid, and cook over a medium heat until all the liquid has been absorbed. Add a ladleful of hot stock to the pan of rice and cook, stirring until absorbed. Continue to add ladles of hot stock at intervals, allowing each addition to be absorbed before adding more, until the risotto is plump, soft and creamy—about 30 minutes. (You may not need to add all the stock.)

Remove the saucepan from the heat and stir in the remaining butter. Season with salt and freshly ground black pepper, then cover and let stand for 2-3 minutes. Serve sprinkled with chopped parsley.

champagne and rose-petal sherbet

A fabulously fragrant dessert with a subtle hint of rose. Use roses that are naturally scented and have not been sprayed.

Syrup:

1¼ cups sugar

1 cup water

6 scented roseheads, washed and petals removed, or 1 tablespoon rosewater

½ bottle of demi-sec Champagne, such as Piper Heidsieck NV

1 egg white, lightly whisked

Serves 4–6

Put the sugar and water in a small saucepan and stir over a low heat until the sugar dissolves. Add the prepared rose petals and bring the mixture to a gentle boil. Reduce the heat and simmer for 10 minutes until a light syrup forms. Remove from the heat and, using a slotted spoon, remove and discard the rose petals. Let syrup cool. For an intense rose flavor, remove petals after syrup has cooled. If using rosewater, add to the cooled syrup.

In a medium bowl, mix the rose-infused syrup, fizz, and lemon juice, then fold in the lightly whisked egg white. Transfer to an ice cream making machine and churn (according to the manufacturer's instructions) until firm. Alternatively, pour the prepared mixture into flat freezer trays and part-freeze to a slush. Using a fork, beat the slush to break up ice crystals, then return to the freezer. Repeat, then freeze until firm. To serve, remove from the freezer and soften in the refrigerator for about 15 minutes, then scoop the sorbet into small bowls or chilled champagne glasses. Best eaten within 2–3 hours of making.

bubbly baked peaches

Fresh, juicy peaches baked in delicious champagne are a winning combination. They taste even better the next day when the flavors have fully developed.

4 large, ripe peaches
½ cup almond ratafia biscuits, crushed
½ cup flaked almonds, lightly toasted and roughly chopped
3 tablespoons light brown sugar
2 tablespoons sweet butter, plus extra for greasing
⅔ cup demi-sec champagne, such as Louis Roederer Riche NV
light whipping cream, whipped, to serve

Serves 4 or 8

Cut the peaches in half and remove and discard the stones. Using a teaspoon, scoop out some of the flesh from the cavity in the peaches, then coarsely chop the bits. Put the chopped peaches, crushed ratafia biscuits, chopped almonds, and sugar in a bowl and mix well.

Put the peach halves in a lightly buttered, shallow baking dish and fill the hollowed-out centers with the almond and peach mixture. Dot the tops with butter and pour the fizz over.

Bake, uncovered, in a preheated oven at 350°F for 35-40 minutes, until the peaches are soft and tender, but still retain their shape, and the liquid has become syrupy. Remove from the oven and let cool slightly. Serve warm, with a little of the syrup spooned over and lashings of whipped cream. Alternatively, cover with plastic wrap and chill overnight for the flavors to fully develop. Remove the chilled peaches from the refrigerator and let stand at room temperature for about 20 mintures before serving with the syrup and cream.

champagne sabayon

The French version of the Italian classic Zabaglione, made with champagne instead of marsala. Spoon into tall glasses and serve with ice cream wafers, or serve poured over lightly poached fruit such as apricots, cherries, peaches, or nectarines.

6 egg yolks
1 cup superfine sugar
¼ bottle brut fizz, such as Freixenet Cordón Negro NV
Serves 6

Put the egg yolks and sugar in a medium-sized mixing bowl and, using a balloon whisk or electric hand-held beater, whisk vigorously until thick and creamy. Bring a saucepan of water to a boil, reduce the heat to barely simmering, then set the bowl over the pan. Check the water level—the bowl and water must not touch. Drizzle in the fizz as you whisk and continue whisking for about 15 minutes until the mixture is thick, fluffy, and doubled in volume. Remove from the heat and serve immediately.

poached apricots

Apricots, peaches, nectarines, and cherries—when in season— are ideal for poaching in a light sugar syrup. Choose one of these or a combination to gently poach, then serve hot or at room temperature with champagne sabayon.

Poaching syrup:
3 tablespoons sugar
1¼ cups water

1 lb. apricots, peaches or nectarines, halved and stones
   removed, or cherries, left whole
Serves 6

In a small saucepan, dissolve the sugar in the water over a low heat. Let boil for about 5 minutes until light and syrupy, then reduce the heat and add the fruit. Cook for about 10 minutes until the fruit is soft but still holds its shape. Transfer the poached fruit and syrup to a serving bowl. Serve hot or let cool, then serve.

champagne truffles

Velvety smooth chocolates that melt in the mouth are a perfect
after-dinner treat with a cup of fine coffee. It is important to use a
good-quality unsweetened chocolate containing about 70 percent
cocoa solids. White chocolate will also make excellent truffles.
Vary the coating if you wish and roll the ganache in finely
chopped nuts or confectioner's sugar, or dip in melted chocolate.

Champagne ganache:
10 oz. unsweetened chocolate or white chocolate, finely chopped
¾ cup heavy cream
2 tablespoons sweet butter, softened
3-4 tablespoons champagne, such as Lanson Black Label Brut NV

Coating, choose from:
good-quality, unsweetened cocoa powder
confectioner's sugar
pistachio nuts, finely chopped
unsweetened chocolate or white chocolate, melted
Makes about 20-30 truffles

To make the ganache, melt the chocolate in a bowl set over a saucepan of hot (not simmering water). Pour the cream into a small saucepan and bring it to a boil. Remove from the heat and pour the hot cream onto the melted chocolate. Using a wooden spoon, stir until thoroughly mixed, then add the softened butter and champagne. Stir well to form a lump-free mixture. Let cool, then cover and chill in the refrigerator overnight.

Using two teaspoons, form the chilled ganache into 20-30 balls and as they are shaped, put onto a baking tray lined with wax paper. Chill the mixture if it becomes too soft to shape.

To coat, put the cocoa, confectioner's sugar or chopped nuts in a bowl. Drop in the truffles, one at a time, and roll to coat. If coating with melted chocolate, freeze the truffle balls for 1 hour, then dip each one into the chocolate and coat well. Remove and let dry on a wire rack. Eat immediately or chill for up to 10 days.

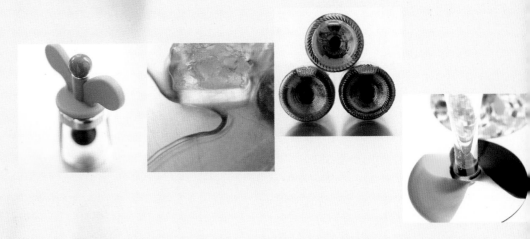

enjoying fizz

serving fizz

storing fizz

Fizz is a delicate and sensitive wine that will spoil if it is poorly stored. If you are going to keep fizz for more than two months it is best to store it in total darkness, undisturbed, and at a constant temperature. Nonvintage champagne benefits from six to eight months of storage—it tastes richer and creamier. Always keep the bottles lying on their side, so that the cork stays wet at all times, otherwise it will dry out and shrink. Don't worry if you haven't got a cellar for short-term storage; under the bed in the spare room where the heating is turned off, or in a cupboard that is seldom opened will be fine. What is important is maintaining a steady temperature with little fluctuation. For long-term storage of one year or more, a cellar or basement is essential.

chilling fizz

Fizz always tastes best well chilled, but the exact temperature for chilling is a matter of personal taste. Three to four hours in the refrigerator is fine, or if you are caught unprepared, a 30-minute blast in the freezer will do the trick. A word of cautionary advice; don't forget about the bottle in the freezer—if the fizz freezes, the cork will shoot out and quite possibly the bottle will explode—I know, I've done it! If you are using an ice bucket, ice mixed with water will cool the fizz much faster than ice alone. Chilling fizz helps reduce the pressure inside the bottle so that it is easier and safer to open, and there is no wastage.

opening the bottle

To open a bottle correctly, take the foil off the top of the bottle, then place the thumb of your left hand on top of the cork and gently untwist the wire cage with your right hand. You can remove this completely, or leave it on. Point the bottle away from your body. Grasp the cork with the palm of your left hand, hold the bottle in your right hand, and gently twist the bottle while holding the cork still. As long as the bottle has not been shaken, the cork should come out quite easily with a gentle pop and a line of smoke-like haze escaping from the bottle. It's a good idea to have a champagne flute or saucer glass at the ready, so that you can capture those all-important bubbles if any do escape.

I experienced a far more dramatic way of opening a bottle of champagne while visiting Canard-Duchêne at Rilly-La-Montagne. I was given a very large sword and shown how, if you tap (quite hard) the neck of the bottle, just below the cork in exactly the right place with just the right amount of force, you can open the bottle by making a clean break through the glass. I was amazed when I managed to open the wine successfully in this fashion, and to this day I still cherish the glass top, cork, and wire intact.

pouring fizz

If you are only serving a few glasses of fizz, it is easiest to tilt the glass first, as you would when pouring beer, so that when you pour it, the glass doesn't overflow with froth. But if you are pouring fizz for a big party, it is best to first pour a little fizz into each glass, to fill by one-third; then as soon as the froth has died down, top up the glasses. If it looks as if the foam will shoot over the top of the glass, quickly put your finger in the middle of the foam or dip the end of a teaspoon handle in the middle.

gadgets

I look at gadgets as optional extras, because the essential ingredients in a fabulous fizz fan's kit are simply a bottle of fizz, two glasses, and someone special to share them with. However, there are many pieces of equipment that you may, on occasion, find useful. One of these is a bottle stopper, a very handy tool to temporarily plug an opened bottle to keep champagne or sparkling wine fizzy. Really good stoppers, like the chrome two-levered one, can keep fizz at its best for up to two weeks. If you are planning to finish the fizz within a day of opening the bottle, try the old trick of putting a teaspoon handle in the neck of the opened bottle. I've no idea why it works, but it does.

For particularly stubborn corks, a pair of champagne pincers (they look like nutcrackers) can make opening bottles much easier, especially if you're opening a number of them. Another particularly good device, known as the Champagne Star, fits neatly over the top of the cork and is simply twisted to release the cork.

Swizzle sticks, like the Cartier one pictured left, are fun to stir cocktails with, but should never be used for fizz or this will render the wine flat. While there were periods in history when this was desirable, it is not considered appropriate today.

Stylish champagne ice buckets always look good and serve to keep the fizz cool before and after the bottle has been opened. A silver ice bucket is traditional, but something novel like the bright orange Veuve Clicquot bucket (see page 32) has a modern feel.

glasses

I am frequently asked the question "what is the best glass for fizz?" The short answer is, whatever style of glass you like, or more practically, the glass nearest to hand! However, custom dictates that certain drinks are more appropriately served in certain glasses, and your enjoyment of that drink will be affected by the size, shape and character of the glass. For fabulous fizz, I much prefer a fine, thin glass, because it feels better in the hand and at the mouth, and somehow it seems the perfect vessel to retain delicate bubbles.

English Georgian champagne glasses, mainly fluted in shape and very finely cut or engraved, are among some of the finest glassware. The Georgian glasses pictured here form part of my father's glass collection and are used regularly on family occasions.

The champagne saucer glass, also known as a coupe, is another traditional glass. It is a stemmed glass with a wide saucer-shaped bowl. It is thought to have been invented in the 17th century and rumored to have been modeled on the left breast of Marie Antoniette! Fact or fiction, it makes an interesting story. Many early coupes had hollow stems, with a tiny pin-prick of glass at the bottom to keep the bubbles fizzing continually up the stem. This style of glass became very fashionable during the Victorian period and again in recent years. Today's modern copies also have hollow stems. Part of the attraction of the hollow-stemmed glass is that in order to drink the last precious drop of fizz, you need to throw your head right back, rather like you do when you laugh raucously!

Contemporary champagne glasses differ from the more traditional kind. They are usually tall flutes, many of which are slightly tulip-shaped so that the aromas from the fizz become concentrated beneath your nose when you take a sip.

Today there is an eclectic mix of champagne glasses to choose from, ranging from the machine-blown variety to the more hedonistic (and of course, more expensive) special hand-blown beauties, and from very plain to highly decorated.

Clear glass tends to be favored among professional wine tasters and producers, purely because it is easier to assess the color of the fizz and its "mousse" (the size and amount of bubbles).

It is important that all glassware is scrupulously clean and polished. Hold the glass up to the light to check for cleanliness and, if necessary, buff the glass with a fine linen cloth, then check again. It is not advisable to wash sparkling wine glasses in detergent since any soap residue will substantially reduce the bubbles in the fizz—if you're a serious fizz fan, nothing will disappoint you faster than a glass of flat fizz.

bottle sizes

Champagne comes in many bottle sizes. The most popular party-size is the magnum—perfect for weddings, christenings, anniversaries, and birthdays. Large bottles, from jeroboams to nebuchadnezzers, are spectacular but not practical unless you have someone very strong to help with the pouring as they are extremely heavy to lift and handle. Bottles are usually green and made with heavy, thick glass to withstand the trapped pressure. The colored glass protects the precious, light-sensitive fizz.

quarter bottle

Ideal for one large glass. Don't keep it hanging around as the wine in this bottle goes bad quite rapidly. Apart from being served on airlines, the quarter bottle became *de rigueur* at haute couture fashion parties in London in the 1990s. Many cutting-edge designers served their guests quarter bottles of Moët, complete with straws!

half bottle

Ideal for one or an abstemious tipple for two. Fizz tends to mature much faster in half bottles so make sure you don't keep them in storage for too long.

bottle (0.75 liters)

Standard bottle size which holds 750 ml of champagne. Ideal for small-scale celebrations.

magnum (1.5 liters)

Contains two standard bottles. Perfect for dinner parties and every kind of celebration. Also, the best size for champagne that is to be aged for a long period.

jereboam (3 liters)

Impressively large bottle containing the equivalent of four standard bottles. This is sometimes referred to as a double magnum.

rehoboam (4.5 liters)

Sometimes known as a triple magnum, this contains the equivalent of six bottles. Relatively few are produced by champagne companies. Big bottles are always a brilliant talking point at any party or celebration.

methusalem (6 liters)

This bottle contains the equivalent of eight standard bottles. Great for special occasions or thirsty guests!

salmanazar (9 liters)

These big bottles contain the equivalent of 12 standard bottles.

balthazar (12 liters)

Large bottles containing the equivalent of 16 standard bottles.

nebuchadnezzar (15 liters)

The biggest available bottle size of champagne, equivalent to 20 standard bottles. The ultimate "show-off" bottle. Extremely heavy to lift and difficult to pour successfully.

index

acknowledgments

Picture Credits
p.14 *left and center left inset* Mick Rock, Cephas; **p.16** *top left* courtesy of Bollinger; **p.16** *below left* Hulton Getty, *right* taken from a poster by Jean de'Ylen published in 1921—courtesy of Joseph-Perrier; **p.17** courtesy of Mumm; **p.20** *right* Maurice Huser, Tony Stone Images; **pp.20–21** Michael Busselle, Tony Stone Images; **p.20** *left and left center inset* Mick Rock, Cephas.

With thanks to Belinda and Guy Battle and everyone else who allowed us to photograph in their homes.

Acknowledgments
My grateful thanks to members of the wine trade who supplied bottles of champagne and sparkling wine as well as information for this book. Special thanks are due to Vicky Bishop, Fiona Campbell, Susie Harris, Gilly Mackwood and from the California Wine Institute, John MacLaren. I would also like to thank my father, Dominic King, for the loan of his beautiful Georgian glasses and my agent Caryl Skelton. Thanks also to Peter Cassidy, who made the images come alive through his sensational photographs that far surpassed anything I could have imagined, and to my dear friend, Amanda Searle, for taking my photograph.

A big thank you to all the team at Ryland Peters & Small for their hard work in putting this book together so beautifully, and especially to Anne Ryland who gave me the opportunity to write *Fabulous Fizz* and Louise Leffler who designed such a wonderful book. And last but not least, thanks to Sally Lester who typed the manuscript and without whom this book could not have been written.

The publishers and author would like to thank all the champagne houses who so generously gave bottles of fizz for photography and to the following companies who loaned the glassware, cutlery, crockery, table linen and accessories that appear in the book:

Asprey & Garrard
167 New Bond Street
London W1
44 171 493 6767

The Conran Shop
81 Fulham Road
London SW3
44 171 589 7401

EGG
16 Kinnerton Street
London SW1
44 171 235 9315

Nicole Farhi Homestore
17 Clifford Street
London W1
44 171 287 8787

Thomas Goode
19 South Audley Street
London W1
44 171 499 2823

Heals
196 Tottenham Court Road
London W1
44 171 636 1666

Michael Johnson Ceramics
81 Kingsgate Road
London NW6
44 171 624 2493
UK distributors for Reidel glasses

Ruffle & Hook
122 St Johns Street
London EC1
44 171 490 4321